THE AGRARIAN REVOLUTION IN GEORGIA
1865-1912

BY

ROBERT PRESTON BROOKS, Ph. D.

Assistant Professor of History
University of Georgia

Sometime Instructor in History
The University of Wisconsin

A THESIS SUBMITTED FOR THE DEGREE OF DOCTOR OF PHILOSOPHY
THE UNIVERSITY OF WISCONSIN

NEGRO UNIVERSITIES PRESS
WESTPORT, CONNECTICUT

Originally published in 1914
by the University of Wisconsin, Madison, Wisconsin

Reprinted in 1970 by
Negro Universities Press
A Division of Greenwood Press, Inc.
Westport, Connecticut

Library of Congress Catalogue Card Number 73-129939

SBN 8371-1603-1

Printed in the United States of America

CONTENTS

CHAPTER I

General Conditions in Georgia, 1865–1870

CHAPTER II

The Failure of the Plantation System

CHAPTER V

THE MOUNTAIN COUNTIES AND THE UPPER PIEDMONT: ECONOMIC HISTORY AND LAND TENURE MOVEMENTS

CHAPTER VI

THE BLACK BELT: ECONOMIC HISTORY AND LAND TENURE MOVEMENTS

CHAPTER VII

THE WIREGRASS COUNTRY AND THE COAST COUNTIES; ECONOMIC HISTORY AND LAND TENURE MOVEMENTS

PREFACE

The economic and social history of the South since the Civil War is an attractive field to the student of American history. In broad outline the changes are well-known—the destruction of the old order of master and slave, the fall of the plantation system, the rise of the former slaves to the position of free laborers, tenants, and landowners, and the economic emancipation of the non-slaveholding class. But the successive steps in this agrarian revolution have not thus far been worked out in detail for any Southern state. The scope of this monograph and the plan of treatment are indicated in the table of contents. Chapters I, II, and III trace the changes in agricultural organization; chapter IV describes the workings of the two principal forms of tenancy that took the place of the plantation-gang system, and the remainder of the study is devoted to an account of present-day labor conditions in Georgia. The state embraces several areas differing widely in physiography and soils, economic history, and character of population. Each of the five divisions is here treated as a distinct unit, making possible interesting contrasts between those parts of Georgia where whites predominate, and those in which negroes outnumber whites.

In the preparation of the historical chapters, I, II, and III, I had the guidance of Professor Carl Russell Fish, in whose seminar in American History at The University of Wisconsin these chapters were presented as reports. Grateful acknowledgments are also due to Professor Henry C. Taylor, of Wisconsin, and Professor U. B. Phillips, of Michigan, who not only lent me valuable unpublished material, but read and criticised the entire manuscript. Professors Frederick L. Paxson and George Clark Sellery, of Wisconsin, also kindly read parts of the manuscript and made useful suggestions as to arrangement of material.   R. P. BROOKS.

Athens, Ga.

1913.

THE AGRARIAN REVOLUTION IN GEORGIA
1865-1912

CHAPTER I

ECONOMIC AND SOCIAL CONDITIONS, 1865–70

The upheaval of the sixties, while leaving untouched no phase of economic and social life in Georgia, necessarily accomplished its profoundest work in connection with the agricultural interest since more than three-fourths of the population was engaged in farming. Agriculture, along with all other industries, suffered from the destruction of capital[1] and loss of

---

[1] Money estimates of the cost of the War are of little value. The subject is beset with many difficulties and it is easier to point out the errors in such calculations than it is to defend one's own figures. It need only be said that the state was practically bankrupt and industry at a standstill. The withdrawal of thousands of men from productive enterprise and the losses resulting from such interruption of the industries of peace, the constant drain on the resources of the state for armies in the field, heavy taxation during and after the war, are items difficult to estimate. The freeing of slaves, while not a social loss of wealth, since their labor remained, entailed loss of credit, disturbance of land titles, and disorganization of labor. Georgia was exempt from actual invasion until near the close of the struggle. Sherman's work, however, was thorough, and it was many years before the section of the state traversed by his army recovered. In his official report, Sherman said : "I was thereby left with a well-appointed army to sever the enemy's only remaining railroad communications eastward and westward, for over 100 miles—namely, the Georgia State Railroad, which is broken up from Fairburn Station to Madison and the Oconee, and the Central Railroad, from Gordon clear to Savannah, with numerous breaks on the latter road from Gordon to Eatonton and from Millen to Augusta, and the Savannah Gulf Railroad. We have also consumed the corn and fodder in the region of country thirty miles on either side of a line from Atlanta to Savannah, as also the sweet potatoes, cattle, hogs, sheep and poultry, and have carried away more than ten thousand horses and mules, as well as a countless number of their slaves. I estimate the damage done to the State of Georgia and its military sources at one hundred millions of dollars, at least twenty millions of which have inured to our advantage, and the remainder is simple waste and destruction." *War of the Rebellion*, Series I, XLIV, p. 13.

credit entailed by the war, to say nothing of the disastrous aftermath of Reconstruction. Peculiar ills, however, affected the planting element, such as an almost total failure of crops in 1865 and 1866; labor difficulties, due to the negroes' misconception of the meaning of liberty; and the extraordinary mobility of the population. Many thousands of people migrated in the sixties and seventies from Middle and North Georgia to the southwestern corner of the state, or to the West. The freedmen, attracted by stories of high wages, departed in large numbers for Mississippi and Louisiana, making it difficult for the Georgia planter to secure labor.

The outlook was distinctly discouraging to the farmers when they returned home in the spring of 1865. During their absence in the armies, the farms had been allowed to run down. Ditches had filled, their banks had grown up with bushes and briers, fences were falling, gates and bars were out of repair; "the teams were ruined by old age and hard usage, and by the constant military impressment system, both officially and without authority, by day and by night,[2]" the farm equipment of plows, hoes, and harrows was worn out. The laborers were in a thoroughly demoralized condition. Cotton was extremely high and everybody turned at once to cotton planting. Good seed were not to be had. The soil was badly prepared and inadequately cultivated; the harvest was a failure, both in 1865 and 1866. Unusually bad seasons during the two years only made matters worse.

So widespread was the distress following the crop failures that thousands of Georgians must have perished from starvation but for the timely aid of the government. The Federal authorities opened a food distributing office in Atlanta in 1865. Thirty-five thousand persons in the counties around that city were dependent upon public aid during the winter of that year.[3] Scarcity of food everywhere in the state was reported by a Chicago *Tribune* reporter who toured Georgia that fall.[4] The

---

[2] *Southern Cultivator* (Athens, Ga.), July, 1867.

[3] *Annual Cyclopedia*, 1865, p. 392. Several interesting letters from Georgia, giving details as to the destitution in North Georgia and the operations of the distributing office at Atlanta.

[4] Andrews, S., *The South Since the War* (Boston, 1866), p. 377.

legislature in March, 1866, appropriated $200,000 to buy corn for the poor.[5] The Commissioner of the Freedmen's Bureau reported for the year 1866 [6] that the crops had been so poor on account of the drought that the farmers were unable to pay their laborers. In the month of September, 1866, 13,758 freedmen and 38,568 whites received aid from the government. During the fifteen months preceding September 1, 1866, the number of "rations" issued by the Bureau in Georgia was 847,694, of which 172,998 were to whites. Comment having been made on the fact that in some months a larger number of whites than freedmen received aid from the Bureau, it was pointed out that much of the food given to whites was by them redistributed to their laborers.

The destitution continued in 1867, but by 1868 conditions had improved, and there was no general issue of food by the Federal government that year.[7]

Farmers who had mortgaged their property to obtain stock, implements, and food with which to make crops were now in desperate straits. Notwithstanding the high price of cotton, the total failure of crops made it impossible for them to meet obligations. Foreclosures were numerous. The debtor class, always ready to demand legislative aid, secured the passage of homestead and exemption acts, removing from the reach of creditors a certain amount of property. Early in 1866 [8] a bill of this sort was vetoed by the governor and the House refused to join the Senate in passing it over the veto; but the movement was a popular one, and the Constitutional Convention of 1868 put into the new constitution [9] an article directing that a homestead of realty to the value of "$4,000 in specie, and personal property to the value of $1,000 in specie, be set apart for each head of a family, or guardian or trustee of a family of minor children." Foreseeing the popular ratification of this constitution, creditors began rapidly to foreclose mortgages. The cry of oppression was raised and General

---

[5] Georgia Comptroller General, *Report*, 1866, p. 21.

[6] 39th Congress, 2nd session, *House Executive Documents*, 3, No. I, pp. 738-9.

[7] 40 Cong., 3 sess., *House Ex. Docs.*, 3, No. I, p. 1044.

[8] Georgia Legislature, *Senate Journal*, 1865-66, pp. 598-9.

[9] Irwin, D., *Code of Georgia Laws*, 1873, p. 925, Sec. 5135.

Meade, then military governor, was induced to declare the acts of the convention binding until passed on by the people.[10]

Since the purpose of this chapter is to picture briefly the abnormal conditions which characterized the transition from the old to the new regime, and in a measure gave to the readjustment of race relations the direction it finally took, it becomes necessary to consider the freedman's conduct in his new status. This was, of course, the most interesting and important of contemporary problems. Public documents, political addresses, diaries, and letters of newspaper correspondents are full of the subject. Opinions as to the negro's capacity for exercising the privileges of freedom vary with the personal and sectional bias of the observers. Southern farmers were, on the whole, convinced that his utility as a laborer had been permanently destroyed. One of the military governors of Georgia, General Pope, was much impressed with the progress the blacks were making. In an official report he expressed the opinion that within five years the bulk of the intelligence of Georgia would be shifted to the negroes. The matter seemed otherwise to a special agent of the American Union Committee, who made a journey through Georgia in 1866. He reported[11] that the negroes as a class "appear to be idle, vagrant, thieving and licentious. They congregate about cities in hosts. A great many live on the resources of the Bureau for Refugees and Freedmen, a great many on small short jobs and pilfering, a few on constant, manly labor . . . I found their general idea of freedom to be, naturally enough, idleness and license."

On many plantations operations went ahead with scarcely any interruption.[12] Planters called informal meetings of the

---

[10] 40 Cong., 3 sess., *House Ex. Docs.*, 3, pt. I, No. I, p. 75.

[11] *DeBow's Review*, May, 1866.

[12] Leigh, Francis Butler, *Ten Years on a Georgia Plantation Since the War* (London, 1883), pp. 14 and 21. "The negroes seem perfectly happy at getting back to the old place and having us there, and I have been deeply touched by many instances of devotion on their part." *Southern Cultivator*, April, 1866, quotes Macon (Ga.) *Telegraph*: "As a general rule, the freedmen, notwithstanding the absurd reports calculated to deter them from entering into agreements, have gone to work with alacrity to earn a livelihood for themselves and families."

freedmen, explained in simple terms their new condition and offered employment at the current rate of wages to all who desired to remain. After wandering off a short distance simply to assert their freedom, many negroes returned to the familiar surroundings and took up their former labor. Those planters who had been most considerate of their slaves experienced the least trouble in employing them as freedmen. This peaceful readjustment seems to have been common during the period of the Johnson governments, although it was in many cases disturbed by the political troubles accompanying the congressional reconstruction.

On the other hand, there was a large element of the freedmen who did not follow the course just outlined. The widespread belief that the plantations of their former owners would be divided among the ex-slaves at Christmas, 1865, acted as a deterrent to steady industry. The Commissioner of the Freedmen's Bureau found it necessary to send out special instructions to all officers and agents, directing them to do what they could to dispel this delusion.[13]

Vagrancy and lawlessness in the towns increased to such an extent as to threaten the stability of society. The correspondent of *The Nation* wrote from Macon that the presence and conduct of negro troops were responsible for a large part of the disorder.[14] Agricultural operations almost ceased in some sections. Governor Jenkins in his annual message of 1867 attributed the crop failures of the past two years in part to the indisposition of the negroes to work. Some sort of repressive measures were necessary. In 1866 the legislature passed laws intended to check vagrancy. One law dealt with vagrants of age,[15] authorizing imprisonment, upon conviction, for a year,

[13] 39 Cong., 1 sess., *House Ex. Docs.* no. 70, p. 34.
[14] *The Nation*, Oct. 5, 1865.
[15] Georgia Legislature, *Acts*, 1865–66, p. 234. "All persons wandering or strolling about in idleness, who are able to work and who have no property to support them; all persons leading an idle, immoral or profligate life, who have no property to support them, and are able to work and do not work . . . shall be deemed and considered vagrants, and shall be indicted as such . . . and upon conviction they shall be fined or imprisoned or sentenced to work on the public roads, for not longer than a year, or shall in the discretion of the court, be bound out to some person for a time not longer than one year, upon such valuable con-

or permitting the county court to bind the vagrant to some person for twelve months. At the same time an apprentice act [16] was passed, providing for the binding out until the age of twenty-one of negro minors whose parents were unable to support them. The master was bound to teach the apprentice some useful occupation, furnish him with wholesome food and clothing, teach him habits of industry, honesty, and morality, cause him to be taught to read English, and govern him with humanity, "using only the same degree of force to compel his obedience as a father may use with his minor children."

No one with any knowledge of negro characteristics can now question the wisdom of such acts, but in the inflamed condition of public opinion in 1866, the laws were widely denounced. It is significant that the Freedmen's Bureau itself recognized the necessity of an apprentice act. Bureau agents in all counties were authorized to bind out minors of both sexes until they were of age. Such contracts were legalized by the legislature.[17]

Arson, burglary, and horse stealing became so prevalent as to lead the legislature to impose the death penalty for these crimes.[18] Minor offenses, such as carrying weapons, driving overseers from plantations, resenting the exercise of legitimate authority, and general disrespect to employers, were rife.[19] Petty misdemeanors, formerly punished by slave owners, now came before the courts, and it became necessary to reduce the penalty attaching to larceny in order to make the punishment more in accord with the untutored condition of the freedmen. The lessening of the penalty for minor infractions of law, in connection with the heightening of the punishment for arson

---

sideration as tɔe court may prescribe; the person giving bond in a sum not exceeding three hundred dollars, payable to said court, and conditioned to clothe and feed and provide said convict with medical attendance for, and during said time."

[16] *Ibid*, p. 6.
[17] *Ibid*, p. 141.
[18] *Ibid*, p. 232.
[19] 42 Cong., 2 sess., *House Reports of Committees*, "*Georgia*," I, p. 305. Testimony of Gen. John B. Gordon before the Ku Klux investigating committee.

Leigh, *Ten Years*, p. 131. During the period of the Congressional Reconstruction, the negroes refused to doff their hats to Mrs. Leigh or to employ titles of respect. They loafed about with guns on their shoulders and worked only when it suited their convenience.

and burglary at night, were admirably suited to existing conditions.

The flood of convicts under the new laws was so great that the central penitentiary was speedily overtaxed. In 1869 the leasing of convicts to private individuals and corporations was begun, a system which developed many objectionable features, although vested interests prevented its abolition until 1908.

It is unnecessary to go into details here as to the ill effects of the congressional reconstruction policy. Suffice it to say that the policy of the congressional radicals fostered and encouraged political rather than industrial activity on the part of the blacks, and thus tended to prevent a speedy and satisfactory readjustment of the labor situation.

In comparison with the middle western states and some of the eastern states, the population of Georgia was relatively stable in the years immediately following the War. But it is easy to overemphasize this tendency to stability. The absence of free government land and the prevalence of political and social troubles rendered Georgia unattractive to immigrants. Such population movement as there was confined itself on the one hand, to migration away from the state, and, on the other, to removals of Georgians from North and Middle Georgia to the southwestern part of the state. This latter movement is shown by maps [20] constructed to indicate the increase or decrease in population by counties between the censuses of 1860 and 1870. The first map, showing the movement of whites, indicates that the counties of extreme South and Southwest Georgia were receiving the bulk of the population leaving the old slave counties, such as Warren, Hancock, Baldwin, Jones, Elbert, and Meriwether. The map showing the shifting of the negro population reveals striking changes. In forty-one counties there was an absolute loss of negroes. These counties lay in three distinct sections. The first was the mountainous region of extreme North Georgia. There had never been many slaves in this region, as it was unsuited

[20] See *App.*, pp. 125, 126.

to agriculture of the sort that made slavery profitable. The freedmen, therefore, migrated to the rich cotton lands further south. The second section was the old cotton belt, in which the lands were worn, the per acre product of cotton low, and consequently wages below the level of the newer regions. The third section that was losing its negro population was the seaboard. There the labor of the slaves had been most arduous on the rice plantations. The negroes refused to do the heavy ditching and banking, and the rice plantations fell into ruins.[21]

Nearly all the counties that received heavy accessions of negroes lay below the fall line of the rivers. This line extends from Richmond County, on the Savannah River, through Baldwin and Bibb Counties, to Muscogee County, on the Chattahoochee. In other words, it was the Piedmont that was losing its population to the coastal plain. The southwestern section is a country of great fertility. It had begun by 1850 to attract planters with their slaves. In that year only two of the counties contained black majorities. By 1860 negroes outnumbered whites in eleven counties. Each succeeding census period has found the proportion of blacks to whites larger in this section.

Three counties in the eastern part of this coastal plain, Pierce, Appling, and Ware, show heavy increases of negroes. These counties were being filled by negroes moving from the coast.[22]

Another noteworthy fact shown by the map is that the cities of Georgia attracted many negroes during the decade. Fulton County, in which is the city of Atlanta, received an increase of 425 per cent., Bibb County (Macon) 80 per cent., Chatham County (Savannah) 60 per cent., Baldwin County (Milledgeville, the capital) 57 per cent., Richmond County (Augusta) 50 per cent.

The effect of these movements of the black population was a thorough disorganization of labor in the older cotton belt, and, in the cities, the introduction of a disorderly and idle element, for whose control the statutes already mentioned were intended.

---

[21] See, *post*, chap. VII.
[22] Leigh, *Ten Years*, p. 156.

The available statistics shed no light on the movement of population away from the state. The Censuses of 1860 and 1870 are of little value in this connection. The Census of 1860 gives no information as to the number of Georgia negroes to be found in other states, so that no comparison can be made in the case of the colored race. Fewer Georgia whites are reported in most of the western states in 1870 than in 1860. Only Texas and Florida appear from the Census returns to have received considerable numbers of Georgians during the decade. Defective returns due to political disturbances are doubtless responsible for this state of affairs. Survivors of the time say that the migration westward was marked, and in the notes of tourists one often comes across such statements as this: "There is a constant drain of emigration from the poorer districts of Georgia . . . . Hundreds of poor Georgians, unable to make a living from the wornout soil, under the new order of things, fly to Texas." [23]

The freedmen, however, were undoubtedly a much less stable element of the population. In 1866 the Comptroller General [24] reported that "the returns for the present year show that the state has lost over one hundred thousand producing laborers since 1863," a fact which he attributed to westward migration and increased mortality among the negroes. A report of the United States Department of Agriculture contains the statement that between 1865 and 1868, 139,988 Georgia negroes had moved west. [25] "For some time," the report states, "the average number (of negroes) passing through Atlanta has been 1,000 daily." The Freedmen's Bureau agent made note of this migration in the report for 1867. [26] In 1867 the average yearly wage paid for farm labor, including rations, was, in Georgia, $125; in Mississippi, $149; in Louisiana, $150; in Arkansas, $136. [27] The negroes were moving, therefore, in response to an economic demand.

---

[23] King, E., *Great South* (Hartford, 1874), p. 366.
[24] Georgia Comptroller General, *Report*, 1866, p. 17.
[25] United States Department of Agriculture, *Yearbook*, 1868, p. 573-574.
[26] 40 Cong., 2 sess., *House Ex. Docs.*, i, No. I, p. 675.
[27] U. S. Department of Agriculture, *Yearbook*, 1867, p. 416.

CHAPTER II

THE FAILURE OF THE PLANTATION SYSTEM

The ante-bellum "plantation" implied large-scale production of a staple crop by forced labor. The success of the system as a productive enterprise lay in the ability of the plantation manager to organize and direct the labor of slaves, over whose movements he had complete control.

The problem confronting the planter in 1865 was to preserve the maximum degree of control over the laborers consonant with their changed condition. The best chance of securing this control seemed to lie in maintaining in most of its essentials the plantation organization. Of what use was the brawn of the masses of freedmen, utterly ignorant and penniless, if dissociated from the intelligence and skill of their former öwners? Let everything proceed as formerly, the contractual relation being substituted for that of master and slave, wages taking the form of money payments instead of consumer's goods, and the laborer's freedom of movement being recognized. With such ideas as these the planters began life anew in 1865. There was no thought of abandoning the direction of labor; all the experience of Georgia cotton producers had taught them that negro laborers would work regularly and efficiently only under the supervision and control of employer or overseer. The plantation was the established form of organization and it was natural that the planters should try to perpetuate it. In 1865, therefore, in a great number of cases all the externals of the former regime were continued: the negroes lived in "quarters", went to the fields at tap of farm bell, worked in gangs under direction, and were rationed from the plantation smokehouse, the charge for food being deducted from the wage. A money wage was usually paid in 1865 and 1866, payment being weekly, monthly, or yearly, according to contract.

Though no definite statement can be made as to the proportion of the planters who attempted to reestablish the plantation system, the evidence indicates that the effort was widespread. Few men now living in Georgia had personal experience in planting in 1865. Only twenty responses were received in reply to a set of questions sent by the writer to men who were farming just after the War.[1] These letters will be referred to as "Inquiries I." Fourteen of the twenty correspondents stated that they attempted in 1865 to continue the plantation system. Exceptions will be noted in a subsequent chapter. The literature of the time abounds in references to attempts to revive the old order.[2]

The high price of cotton in 1865 and 1866 (43.5 cents in 1865; 31.6 in. 1866), was a mighty stimulus to cotton production. Every planter who could assemble a force of laborers went feverishly to work. The result of the operations of 1865 was a bitter disappointment. In spite of the abnormal price of the staple, heavy losses were sustained. The leading southern agricultural journal of the time was *The Southern Cultivator,* published at Athens, Georgia. The issues from 1865 to 1870 are full of letters, communicated articles, and editorials bearing on agricultural conditions. As early as the issue of July, 1865, the wages-plantation system came under fire. It was impossible to get cash to pay wages, for money was simply non-existent in Georgia.[3] The wages fixed by the Freedmen's Bureau were unreasonably high.[4] The labor was worthless in the absence of power to compel

---

[1] Names of responsible planters were obtained from officials of the Farmers' Union of Georgia, from the editor of the principal agricultural journal of the state, from the agricultural college, and from various individuals. Seventy-five sets of questions were sent out. A number were returned with the statement that the addressee was dead.

[2] Leigh, *Ten Years,* p. 56. U. S. Department of Agriculture, *Report,* 1867, p. 419. Letter of B. F. Ward. *Report of the Industrial Commission,* 1900, X, p. 448. Testimony of R. J. Redding, former director of the Georgia Experiment Station. Barrow, David C., in *Scribner's Magazine,* April, 1881.

[3] *Southern Cultivator,* July, 1865, editorial.

[4] *Ibid,* "A man would be absolutely demented to contract with negro labor at any such prices or conditions. . . . When white men, for the time being, are absolutely offering to work for their food alone, and bring to their work not only muscle, but honesty and intelligence, the idea of binding oneself, with no money on hand—with no prospect of getting it in October—and a very dim one of obtaining it at all, to pay negroes these monthly rates, over and above the amount they steal, and, in addition to provide not only food, quarters and fuel, but an indefinite amount of medical attendance—an item no sane man would contract to furnish—and moreover to make no deduction for absence on account of sickness or bad weather, is most perfectly absurd."

attention to duty. The negro saw no reason why he should **not** stop work to go fishing; he was willing to sacrifice his wages and was unconcerned about the state of the crop.[5] The following letter is reproduced as typical of the difficulties experienced in the transitional period by the operator of a plantation:[6]

"Hurricane Plantation, July 31, 1865.

"Accordin to promis I write you to inform you how the negrows **or** freedmen air getting on. tha dont doo as well as tha did a few weeks back. your proposition to hier them has no effect on them at all. tha say and contend that onley three of them agreed to stay that was the three that spoke Sam, Alleck and Johnson. the rest claim tha made no agreement whatever and you had as well sing Sams to a ded horse as to tri to instruct a fool negrow. Some of them go out to work verry well others stay at thier houseses untell an hour by sun others go to thier houseses an stay two an three days. Say ennything to them the reply is I am sick but tha air drying fruit all the time tha take all day evry Satturday without my lief I gave orders last Satturday morning for them to go to work when tha got the order eight went out I ordered tom to go to mill he said he would not doo so. tha air stealing the green corn verry rapped som of them go when tha pleas and wher tha pleas an pay no attention to your orders or mine the commandant of post at milledgeville sent Walker back under Gen Wilson order I exsplained the matter to him but he would send him back unless you had paid him for his work up to the time you ordered him off I told Walker ef he came back he would not get a cent for his work not even his clothes nor those [sic] he cam back in the face of all the orders had ben given him. I drove him off the Secont time after you left before I recieved a written order to take him back I then went down an saw the officer in command and exsplained the hole matter to him but he said he could not allow him driven off without violating Gen Wilsons order an he was compeld to carry them out as such the matter stands as bove stated it would be best for you to visit the plantation soon or write a verry positive letter to be read to them requiering them to work or leave though I think I will get Som of them by not feeding them which proses is now going on though tha is rather two mutch fruit and green corn to have a good effect. I send Alleck up with wagon an mule pleas write back by Alleck I am sick at this time I have had fevor for three days no other matters of importance at present

(Signed) J. D. COLLINS."

[5] *Ibid*, December, 1865.

[6] This letter was written to General Howell Cobb by the overseer of one of his plantations. The original is in the possession of Mrs. A. S. Erwin (a daughter of General Cobb), of Athens, Ga. Copy was furnished by Professor U. B. Phillips, of the University of Michigan, who is now editing the Cobb letters.

The charge of unreliability was made against the negroes in practically every issue of the *Cultivator;* if paid on Saturday, they were as likely to be absent as present on Monday.[7]

After the experience of 1865, the editor of the *Cultivator* suggested the substitution of the share system, hoping that the planters might in this way enlist the self-interest of the negroes in the farming and thus check their roving proclivities. There was no suggestion that this change would in any way impair the owner's control over the labor. Thus, while advocating the share arrangement, the editor said: "There is little hope that this or any other plan will succeed, under any other oversight than the planter's own eye."[8]

It seems that in 1866, on the whole, the negroes improved as laborers.[9] The Freedmen's Bureau was exercising pressure on them, and they had by that time learned that the expected division of lands would not take place. Planters continued to operate the plantation system, though still with discouraging results. General Howell Cobb wrote the following letter from his "Dominie" plantation, on which one Nathan Barwick was overseer.[10] This plantation was in Sumter County, Southwest Georgia, where labor conditions were supposedly better than elsewhere in the State.

"December ——, 1866.

"I find a worse state of things with the negroes than I expected, and am unable even now to say what we shall be able to do. From Nathan Barwick's place every negro has left. There is not one to feed the stock, and on the other places none have contracted as yet. I shall stay here until I see what can be done. By Tuesday we shall probably know what they will do. At all events I shall then look out for other negroes.

---

[7] *Southern Cultivator,* July, 1866. Letter from Greene County, in central Georgia, describing experiences of 1865. The farmer began work with fifteen negroes; one by one they wandered off, until finally in 1866 there were on the place "one woman and two children large enough for light field service. The rest have gone, and may they never return, for while the productive capacities of the farm are greatly diminished, it is at the same time divested of a lawless gang, that by its insolence, its disposition to appropriate to its own use our poultry, our stock, and the remainder of last year's corn and potatoes . . . has lain like a huge incubus on the minds of those having the care of the farm."

[8] *Ibid,* December, 1865.

[9] *Ibid,* April, 1866, quoted Macon *Telegraph* to the effect that the negroes in that section had gone to work with alacrity, and that those farmers who had adopted the share arrangement were the more successful. Similar letters in this issue from Schley County and Columbia County.

[10] Copy lent by Professor Phillips.

I intend to send Nathan Barwick to Baldwin [County] on Wednesday to see what hands can be got there, with the assistance of Wilkerson. I am offering them even better terms than I gave them last year, to-wit, one-third of the cotton and corn crop, and they feed and clothe themselves, but nothing satisfies them. Grant them one thing, and they demand something more, and there is no telling where they would stop. The truth is, I am thoroughly disgusted with free negro labor, and am determined that the next year shall close my planting operations with them. There is no feeling of gratitude in their nature. Let any man offer them some little thing of no real benefit to them, but which looks like a little more freedom, and they catch at it with avidity, and would sacrifice their best friend without hesitation and without regret. That miserable creature Wilkes Flag sent old Ellick down to get the negroes from Nathan Barwick's place. Old Ellick staid out in the woods and sent for the negroes and they were bargaining with him in the night and telling Barwick in the day that they were going to stay with him. The moment they got their money, they started for the railroad. This is but one instance, but it is the history of all of them. Among the number was Anderson, son of Sye and Sentry, whom I am supporting at the Hurricane."

This letter is interesting and important, coming from a planter who was attempting to operate several plantations, widely separated, with resident overseers on each; he was suffering from the great competition among employers for labor; he was becoming disgusted and resolving to abandon planting; and he was supporting ex-slaves too old for work. This competition for laborers was one of the most important reasons of the great changes in the system of farming, subsequently to be described. The movements of the negroes became more general in 1866, and the conviction was growing that a new system must be inaugurated.[11]

The year 1867 found better conditions in some sections, worse in others. In many counties the negroes came under the influence of carpetbag reconstruction; idleness and thievery increased in the towns and cities; migration continued to be the chief complaint. So pronounced became the scarcity of laborers in Middle

---

[11] *Southern Cultivator*, April, 1866, letter from Schley County: "It is evident that an entirely new system of farming (not planting) must be inaugurated in the South." From Columbia County: "I believe, therefore, that there are two duties devolving upon agricultural journals. First, to urge upon farmers the necessity of adopting some plan of cultivation that will dispense with the services of freedmen as far as possible."

Georgia[12] that radical changes in agricultural organization were suggested and carried out. Large plantations in that region lay idle for want of laborers.[13] The planters were confronted with the alternative of totally abandoning their plantations or of taking laborers on their own terms. Some planters under this pressure rented their lands outright to negroes. The editor of the *Cultivator* came out frankly in the November, 1867, issue with the statement that "Under the present state of affairs, experience of the past two seasons has demonstrated that plantations on an extended scale, with free labor, cannot be made profitable. The first change that must occur, and which will eventually prove beneficial, is the subdivision of landed estates." Certain recommendations constantly recur in communications from leading agriculturists of the state, namely, contraction in amount of land used, more intensive culture, manuring, and use of improved implements and commercial fertilizers. The dominant idea underlying these suggestions was the economizing of labor.[14]

Opinion was rapidly shifting by 1868 in favor of abandoning the old system. Letters still appeared in the *Cultivator* advocating the plantation arrangement, but letters of opposite tendency were more numerous. In January, 1868, a long and interesting communication appeared under the caption "The Question of Labor," unsigned, but by a Middle Georgia planter. He advised the retention of the plantation system, maintaining that the trouble in the past two years had arisen from the excessively

---

[12] This is the region from which the greatest exodus of negroes occurred. See map, *post*, p. 126.

[13] *Southern Cultivator*, March, 1867. Letter from Warren County: "We begin to feel the want of laborers in this county, some of our best planters are selling off their stock, not being able to get freedmen to work their land, it is not because they are leaving the county, they are here, we worked in this county a great many large plantations now lying idle in a great measure. I heard of one man renting 2,000 acres to freedmen, and a great many others more or less, whether it is good policy or not, is the question, it has a tendency to keep them with us. But they will almost starve and go naked before they will work for a white man, if they can get a patch of ground to live on, and get from under his control."

[14] *Ibid*, November, 1867. Letter from Floyd County: "We cannot expect to make better crops, and improve our lands, and *economize labor*, unless we get improved implements to cultivate with, and manure to apply to our lands." Another correspondent wrote: "Negro labor is scarce and unreliable, and we must use such tools as will do the most work. I have bought this year two cultivators, a combined reaper and mower, a patent cider press, etc."

high wages and the unreliability and instability of labor. The correspondent stated that planters who had employed negroes in 1867 at from $150 to $200 per annum would not want them in 1868 at half that price, cotton having taken a decided tumble. He ended with a plea that all pull together and regulate wages. In his opinion in Middle Georgia good men were worth $6 per month and board, in Southwest Georgia, $8 and board. "Don't go out to look up hands by any means. Let them hunt homes and they will not be so arrogant and self-inflated. Dictate your own terms to them . . . Let a certain price rule the land throughout." Other planters expressed views diametrically opposed to these. For instance, the May, 1868, *Cultivator* prints the following: "I am satisfied from my experience and close observation for the past two years, there is but one correct mode of working our present labor (which I think is the best in the world), and it is simply this. Let each family work by itself, in separate fields or farms. This is much easier and I think far better than the old plantation style of working all together." On the seacoast matters were in a desperate condition.[15]

The supply of negroes available as wage hands was even less adequate in 1869 than during the preceding year. The West was still drawing away many negroes. But by this time a new complaint became general, namely, that planters were renting their lands to negroes. It is to be carefully noted that migration and renting had exactly the same effect on the planter who was trying to maintain the plantation system. The presence of large numbers of renters indicated that many planters had given up the struggle and abandoned their holdings to negro renters. The case was excellently put by a Burke County planter:[16]

[15] Leigh, *Ten Years*, pp. 128–129. "Everywhere sullenness and unwillingness to work is visible [in 1868], and all around us people are discussing how to get other labourers in the place of negroes. But alas! on the rice lands white labour is impossible, so that I really don't know what we shall do, and I think things look very gloomy for the planters. Our Northern neighbours on St. Simon's, the D——s, who were most hopeful last year, are now perfectly discouraged with the difficulties they have to encounter with their labour, and of course having to lose two or three months every year while the negroes are making up their minds whether they will work or not, obliges us to plant much less ground than we should otherwise do."
[16] *Southern Cultivator*, February, 1869.

"We had more laborers in this neighborhood for 1868 than we had for 1869, and no one knows where it [sic] has gone. A partial explanation is to be found in the fact, that some of the landowners have rented lands to negroes, to farm upon their own responsibility. This is certainly ruinous to the general interest. Those who rent their lands to negroes, never realize any profit, and the negroes never make a support, hence, they steal all the stock within reach—have all the loafing vagabonds in the community around them. *It takes an immense quantity of labor from under the direction of the skillful farmer,* and where four bales of cotton were formerly made to the hand, not one will be made the present year by the negroes, who are working on rented lands."

The significant words have been italicized; it was the escape from skillful direction that was unfortunate from the standpoint of production and conservation.

The supply of labor was said to be steadily diminishing this year also in Southwest Georgia.[17] Of course, the constantly increasing tendency of negro women to withdraw from field work accentuated the scarcity of labor.

Clearly, the plantation system was tottering in 1869, in large measure on account of the inability of planters to secure the necessary labor. Had the blacks been willing to work as hired day laborers, it is probable that the plantation would have been widely preserved, for those planters who were efficient managers and were able to find laborers succeeded in maintaining themselves under the new conditions. There were more of such cases than has been supposed. The most active and determined planters, with ranks recruited from the former overseer class, continued very much on the former lines. Indeed, there has never been a time up to the present when excellently ordered and successful plantations have not existed in the black belt counties. Only the most vigorous men succeed in the planter's rôle. A convention, presumably of such men, held in Atlanta in 1869, was unanimously of the opinion that the old system was the best.[18] Nordhoff, in 1875, observed[19] that the best planters in Georgia preferred the wage system. But the conditions of success were

---

[17] *Ibid.* Article copied from Cuthbert *Appeal* [Randolph County].
[18] Milledgeville [Ga.] *Southern Recorder,* February 9, 1869.
[19] Nordhoff, Charles, *Cotton States in the Spring and Summer of 1875* (New York, 1876), p. 107.

hard—too exacting for the general run of the ante-bellum type of planter. Even where laborers were to be had, the task of supervising their efforts was one requiring almost superhuman endurance and talents of a high order. A Baldwin County (Middle Georgia) overseer writes thus of his methods:[20]

"I am in my seventy-eighth year . . . I am now attending to the business part of a farm for another man . . . I have 21 hands all told . . . I get up at three o'clock, make my own fire, having the wood at hand, sit by it and think over my day's business, come to my conclusions, ring the bell twenty minutes before day, for all hands to rise, the women go to cooking for breakfast and dinner, get off to work before sunrise, every set of hands have their work for the day told them. I have quite early breakfast, saddle and mount my little mule and am with the hands or going from one set to another until the middle of the day, come home, get dinner and go off again frequently in less than an hour."

It was a hard matter to find men like this who were willing to work as overseers. With such capacity for work, and plenty of land to be had at nominal prices, they quickly set up for themselves. The fathers of some prominent citizens of Georgia today were once overseers on slave plantations. The reward awaiting their skill and industry was great and they seized the opportunity. Those planters who were less proficient in the art of managing negroes, whose methods were slack and who did not stay constantly on the plantation, were forced out of the business.

It should be evident from the foregoing that in trying to maintain the system of large scale production with closely supervised labor, the planters, as a class, were fighting against economic and social forces much too powerful for them to overcome. The first in importance of these forces was the repugnance of the negroes to supervision and their determination to escape from it, coupled with an abundance of very cheap land to which they might resort as tenants. Secondly, the negroes largely controlled the situation in Georgia by virtue of the urgent demand for cotton-producing labor, intensified by the call of the western cotton belt for labor from the East. In the third place, the maintenance of a wage system necessitated the use of considerable sums of cash, and few planters could obtain ready money.

---

[20] *Southern Cultivator*, April, 1866.

To meet this difficulty, lien laws were enacted, by which supplies could be obtained from merchants on the execution of a lien on the coming crop. These laws were at first intended to permit only planters to give crop liens, but subsequent modications extended the privilege to tenants, so that the lien laws facilitated the escape of the negroes from the supervision of the landlord, though substituting a more exacting master, the merchant. These considerations require further elaboration.

It was natural that the negro should desire to control his own movements. His crude conception of freedom was summed up in his release from physical restraint. Rarely beyond the confines of the plantation as a slave, now that he was at liberty to travel, the desire to wander was irresistible. Of course, the plantation system of free hired labor meant almost as much restriction as did slavery. If the negro expected to receive a daily or weekly wage, he had to work every day and work as directed. From daylight to dark was the universal rule on cotton plantations. Where no alternative of working for a share or of renting presented itself, the freedman attempted to preserve his liberty of movement by refusing to hire for a year. He greatly preferred to contract for a week or a month, and in many cases would not contract for more than two days in the week.[21] The presence of the overseer became extremely irksome to the negroes, even where the control was very liberal.[22]

There was, however, no reason why the negroes should remain in the status of wage laborers. They were in a position to make terms for themselves. Each year after 1865 found the planters more and more convinced that they would be unable to preserve the plantation organization. In order to keep the negroes from abandoning the older cotton belt in Georgia for the fertile West or the new Southwest corner of Georgia, it was necessary that wages should be fixed to meet the opportunity element which the negro demanded, or retain him by changing his status to that of tenant, or quasi-tenant. That the difference in the wage offered in Georgia and other cotton states was material is seen from the following table:

[21] U. S. Department of Agriculture, *Yearbook,* 1866, p. 573.
[22] Barrow, in *Scribner's Magazine,* April, 1881.

Comparative Wages in Southern States [23]

	1867	1868
North Carolina	$104	$89
South Carolina	100	93
Georgia	125	83
Florida	139	97
Alabama	117	87
Mississippi	149	90
Louisiana	150	104
Texas	139	130
Arkansas	158	115
Tennessee	136	109

These figures represent the yearly wage in addition to food. It will be noted that in Georgia the break between 1867 and 1868 was sharper than in any other state, a fact which had immediate effect on the labor situation in Georgia.

It is not to be supposed that the horde of ex-slaves would of themselves have responded to such a fluctuation in the rate of wages. External pressure of the most effective sort was supplied. Planters from the West came in numbers, hired gangs of negroes, furnished transportation and took them away from Georgia.[24] The Freedmen's Bureau was most active in this connection. It became a vast intelligence office, supplying planters from all over the South with information as to sources of labor. Through the exertions of the various Commissioners of the Bureau, thousands of negroes were moved from Middle Georgia. Very often the government paid transportation expenses. In 1866 the Assistant Commissioner for Georgia reported[25] that he was "overwhelmed by applications for laborers," and that "the demand for labor and the price paid for it are increasing every day." Bureau agents, scattered over Georgia, kept in correspondence with General Tillson, head of the Bureau in Georgia, and the shifting of laborers in response to the economic demand became a regular feature of bureau activity. For instance, the agent in Southwest Georgia wrote to General Tillson in January, 1866, that there was a great de-

[23] U. S. Department of Agriculture, *Yearbook*, 1876, pp. 130–131.
[24] Trowbridge, J. T., *The South*, 1866, p. 460. "Every day anxious planters from the great valley were to be met with [in Georgia], inquiring for unemployed freedmen or returning home with colonies of laborers."
[25] 39 Cong., 1 sess., *Sen. Ex. Docs.*, 2, no. 27, pp. 88–89.

mand for labor in Baker County and asked that four or five hundred hands be sent. Three to five hundred, he said, were also needed in Dougherty County. "I have engaged two Plantations for your Wilkes County [Middle Georgia] freedmen, are they coming?"[26]

By way of digression, it may be said that but for the interference of the Bureau, the negroes would have been at the mercy of their employers. Exercising under the Federal Law complete supervision over the contractual relations between the races, the officials required that contracts should be in writing and should not be considered binding unless approved by the Bureau. As the officials refused to approve contracts in which the rate of wages was lower than they thought fair, a general rise in wages followed. General Tillson reported that his supervision had increased wages from between two and seven to between ten and fifteen dollars per month.[27] A typical case of such interference was related by General Tillson to Mr. Trowbridge.[28] An Oglethorpe County planter had contracted with laborers at $75 to $100, with food and house, per year. The contract was set aside by the assistant commissioner on the ground that the planter could afford to pay $144, food, and house. The question was argued at length between the two and finally the commissioner requested the planter to make an estimate of the result should he pay $144 per laborer. The planter submitted the following:

"Good hands will make 2 bales (of cotton)................. $300.00
   85 bu. of corn.. 85.00
                                                          _____
                                                          $385.00

Expenses.

3 lbs. Bacon per week at 60c, 1 peck meal per week,
    at 25c $44.20
Rent of cabin......................................   10.00
Fuel 25.00
Wages 144.00
                                                    _____ $223.20

Net profit per man................................. $161.80

---

[26] *Ibid*, pp. 89–90.
[27] *Ibid*.
[28] Trowbridge, *South*, p. 492.

In the unsettled condition of labor, it became a common thing for negroes who had contracted with one planter to be enticed away by promises of higher pay elsewhere.[29]   It was a matter more of chagrin than of surprise if one's entire plantation force disappeared over night.   The negroes were entirely devoid of any conception of the binding nature of a contract, and the conduct of the whites in inducing them to break contracts quite naturally did not tend to enlighten them.   Of course, legal action against the freedman was useless.   The Bureau attempted to stop the practice of enticing laborers by imposing fines.   A Macon County planter was fined $150 for enticing hands in 1865.[30]   In 1866 the legislature[31] made it a misdemeanor to entice another's servant, and it is interesting to note that a law to this effect has been of force ever since.[32]   Under the act of 1866 an important case arose in Lee County, Southwest Georgia, in which a verdict of $5,000 was returned for enticing away thirteen laborers in 1868.[33]

The extremes to which Georgians were sometimes put in order to retain laborers is indicated in the following letter written by a Mississippi planter to Trowbridge:[34]

"I determined to go to Georgia for the purpose of obtaining the requisite number of hands.   I succeeded tolerably well, and could have hired many more than I needed had not the people induced the negroes to believe that we were taking them to Cuba to sell them.   I award the palm to the Georgians as the meanest and most despicable class of people it was ever my misfortune to meet."

The scarcity of labor has been canvassed at such length in order to emphasize the fundamentally important fact in the history of the changes that were to come, namely, the negroes' control over the situation.   In the dilemma between abandoning farming or hiring negroes on their own terms, many planters chose the former alternative.   Their idle plantations, available for the renter, only made it the more difficult for those not dis-

---

[29] 42 Cong., 2 sess., *House Reports of Committees,* "Georgia," 2, p. 758.   Testimony of B. H. Hill before Ku Klux Committee.

[30] Trowbridge, *South,* p. 465.

[31] Legislature of Georgia, *Acts,* 1866, pp. 153–154.

[32] *Ibid,* 1873, p. 20, 1882–83, p. 58, 1901, p. 63.

[33] Milledgeville (Ga.) *Southern Recorder,* April 23, 1872.   Case of West v. Lee.

[34] Trowbridge, *South,* p. 498.

posed to give up, to hire wage hands. Those planters who desired to continue farming were forced to modify the system to suit the wishes of the negroes. The material fall in wages in 1868 in response to the break in cotton prices[35] doubtless had its effect in increasing the negro's desire to escape from the old system. Not understanding the economic causes which fixed wages, and seeing the cotton still being produced, he was of the opinion that he was being defrauded.

The luxury of having their erstwhile owners compete for their services did not make for the economic efficiency of the negroes. General Tillson, a stanch friend of the blacks, was quoted[36] in 1865 as saying that he was satisfied the negroes were not generally doing more than about half the work they might. Dissatisfaction at their predicament of having to pay very high wages for very poor labor led planters to experiment with white laborers from Europe and the North. Irishmen were used on the coast to do banking and ditching on the rice plantations, work which the negroes refused longer to do.[37] In 1873 the Leighs imported English laborers, but they were a failure.[38] The effort to secure labor other than the negro was in line with the experience of other southern states. Coolie labor was favored in Mississippi and Louisiana. The press of the period was full of agitation over the subject of immigration. But the demand was from the planter class for laborers: one rarely sees in the literature of the time inducements held out to foreign or northern farmers. Small tracts of land on easy terms were not often the subject of editorials and communications. It was always the scarcity of wage labor that was stressed. Naturally enough,

---

[35] The average price of cotton for the years 1865 to 1870, inclusive, is given as follows in Hammond, M. B., *Cotton Industry*, in American Economic Association, *Publications*, New Series, No. 1, 1897, app.

1865	83.38c
1866	43.20
1867	31.59
1868	24.85
1869	29.01
1870	23.98

[36] Andrews, *South*, pp. 359–360.

[37] Leigh, *Ten Years*, p. 128. Phillips, U. B., in Documentary History of American Industrial Society, (Cleveland, 1910) *Plantation and Frontier*, II, pp. 181–182.

[38] Leigh, *Ten Years*, pp. 204–206.

the effort to attract immigration on these terms was a dismal failure. It could hardly have been otherwise, when in the West the government was offering quarter sections of virgin land free to the actual settler, in a region where social conditions were much more favorable.

An intelligent non-southern contemporary observer of the conditions prevailing in the South at that time, said in effect that in the settlement of the relations between the white employers and negroes, negroes had whites at a great disadvantage. The demand for labor, emigration of negroes, absence of white labor, the possibility of the negro's living for practically nothing, a foolish lien law, all worked for the negro.[39]

Probably no phase of southern post-bellum agriculture has attracted more attention than the credit system which has grown up around the lien laws. The history and effects of the system over the South at large and in Georgia in particular have already received monographic treatment.[40] So early as December 15, 1866, the Legislature passed an Act[41] permitting landlords to have by special contract in writing "a lien upon the crops of their tenants for such stock, farming utensils, and provisions, furnished such tenants, for the purpose of making their crops," and providing that "factors and merchants shall have a lien upon the growing crops of farmers for provisions furnished and commercial manures furnished." The word "farmer" here was not intended to include tenant farmers. In January, 1873, the law[42] was extended so as to enable merchants to take crop liens from tenants also, but the following year the law[43] was again changed so as expressly to deprive merchants of the right to take crop liens from any but the landlord. The next year, however, the legislation against merchants taking liens from tenants was rendered practically null by an act[44] permitting landlords to assign

[39] Trowbridge, *South*, p. 465.
[40] Hammond, M. B., *op. cit.*, chap. V. Banks, M. M., *Economics of Land Tenure in Georgia* (New York, 1905), chap. III.
[41] Legislature of Georgia, *Acts*, 1866, p. 141.
[42] *Ibid*, 1873, p. 43.
[43] *Ibid*, 1874, p. 18.
[44] *Ibid*, 1875, p. 20. Banks was in error in supposing (*Economics of Land Tenure in Georgia*, pp. 47–48) that the *Act* of Oct. 17, 1891 (*Acts*, 1890–91, I, pp. 72–73) introduced an innovation by declaring in par. 2 "whenever said liens

their liens for supplies, and providing that such assigned liens might be enforced by the assignees in the manner provided for their enforcement by landlords.

These rapid changes in the law indicate a conflict between the planters and the merchants. Planters desired the exclusive right to take liens for supplies from tenants, because they could in this way regulate the expenditures of tenants, and would be justified in exercising supervision over their work in order to protect themselves from loss. Merchants desired to deal directly with tenants because they were easy prey and would buy everything in sight as long as the merchant would extend credit. Tenants preferred to deal directly with the merchants because it increased their sense of importance and enabled them to escape from supervision on the part of the landlord. The Act of 1875 may be regarded as a compromise measure, enabling those planters who were firm enough and sufficiently strong financially, to retain control over their tenants in the matter of supplies; and, on the other hand, legalizing the transfer of the supply lien in cases where the planters desired to escape from the bother of managing the negroes and were willing to abandon the whole business to the merchant.

Here again the difficulties of the planter desiring to preserve his organization were increased. In most cases where the landlord assigned his lien for supplies, thus practically abandoning control over his place, he moved to town and became an "absentee." Negroes at once began to abandon the well-regulated plantations in favor of the merchant-controlled absentee places. The result is simply and adequately stated in one of the letters in "Inquiries I:"[45] "Non-resident land holders rented their land,

---

[for supplies] may be created by special contract in writing, as now provided by law, the same shall be assignable by the landlord, and may be enforced by the assignees in the manner provided for the enforcement of such liens by landlords." This provision was introduced in 1875 (*Acts,* 1875, p. 20), and is given as existing law in Irwin's *Code,* 1882, sec. 1978, 2, p. 473. No statute between 1882 and 1891 repealed this provision. The Act of 1891, which Banks thought introduced the new principle, was intended to amend Code sec. 1978 (Code of 1882) in another particular, and after the amending words were introduced, the revised section was reprinted in full in the Acts of 1891. There were seven paragraphs in this Code section, and only one of them was amended in 1891. The others remained identically the same, among them the one permitting the assignment of liens for supplies.

[45] *Inquiries I,* letter from Putnam County.

forcing those who resided on farm to adopt the rental system or no labor could be procured.''

While the subsequent effects of the lien laws were bad, it cannot be doubted that, at the time they were enacted, they were a boon to the farmers. Only the small minority of planters could borrow money from banks. The masses of cotton producers had no basis of credit except land, which was not a favored form of security with banks. Furthermore, in most cases the loan desired was small and credit for a year's time was needed,—additional reasons why banking of the sort that then existed was of little help. The lien law provided a basis of credit in an emergency when no other relief was practicable. Had the conditions been favorable, the introduction of a cooperative agricultural credit system would have been the salvation of the farming class.

The small town merchant now became a factor in the farming situation. The great cotton factors of the cities were ruined, and the country bank took over the business of supplying the merchants with money. In the early spring, the farmers would call on the merchant, arrange for credit, execute a crop lien, sometimes with the additional security of a real estate or chattel mortgage. He would then procure supplies of tools, clothing, foodstuffs, and commercial fertilizers from time to time as occasion required, and settle the account from the proceeds of his crop at the end of the year.

The lien laws greatly facilitated the transformation of the agricultural system. Two developments took place, both of which involved widespread abandonment of the wage system. One of these changes was the introduction of the share system. The majority of the planters refused to assign their liens for supplies to merchants. They got supplies directly from the merchants and used them to furnish their laborers with their minimum of subsistence, deferring a final settlement to the end of the year, when each individual laborer was paid the value of the cotton raised on the small farm allotted to him, less the cost of his keep. Both planter and laborer were willing to give up the money payments, the planter alarmed at the fall in the price of cotton, and the negro at the sharp drop in wages. Under this share arrangement, subsequently to be described at length, the planter did not by any means give up his right of supervision, but his control was weakened, for when the negro was received into what was virtually a partnership, he was able to assert himself to a greater degree than as a day laborer. Whatever loss from the point of view of production might have been entailed by this change was at least partly offset by the greater stability given to the labor, since the negroes necessarily remained on one farm for at least one year.

The share system may be called "quasi-tenancy," since under it the landlord retains a large measure of control over the labor. The second development was the introduction of real tenancy, or renting. In cases where the landlord would assign his lien for supplies, the tenants received their supplies directly from the merchant, and remained under no control whatever, their only connection with the landlord being the obligation to pay a fixed amount of rent, either in cash or in cotton. Under this renting arrangement, it was necessary that the tenant have sufficient capital to buy stock and tools, or be able to induce some one to "set him up." Those negroes who could do neither of these things became share tenants.

Yet another consequence followed the lien laws. The landpoor planters in many, many cases were willing to sell land at nominal prices to their ex-slaves or to white purchasers of the former non-slaveholding class. The sales were commonly on the basis of deferred payments. The lien laws enabled these new proprietors to stock their farms and operate on credit, with a good chance in prosperous times of paying off the incumbrances on their lands. Negroes in Georgia, in 1874, owned 338,769 acres of land,[46] most of which was doubtless acquired in the above fashion.

But many planters and small farmers were ruined by the lien laws. Exorbitant credit-prices were charged, and a bad crop would prevent the farmer from paying his account, which had to be carried over, with interest, to the following year. A succession of unfavorable seasons, a failure of the labor supply, or bad management, soon involved many hopelessly in debt. Wholesale

---

[46] Du Bois, W. E. B., *Negro Landowner of Georgia*, in U. S. Department of Labor, *Bulletin* no. 35, July, 1901, p. 665.

executions of mortgages followed (mortgages on real estate were commonly given as additional security), and landed estates passed into the hands of the town merchants.[47]   These merchants combined the supply business with farming on the negro tenant plan, looking to the mercantile feature of the relationship for most of their profit.   This system became widespread, and almost prostrated agriculture in the black belt.

---

[47] Banks, *op. cit.*, pp. 49–50.

CHAPTER III

DECADENCE OF PLANTATIONS: BEGINNINGS OF SMALL PROPRIETORSHIPS AND OF TENANCY

The forces which led to the fall of the ante-bellum plantation system having been discussed in the last chapter, an attempt will now be made to bring together from various sources information bearing on the actual process of the disintegration of the plantations, and the subsequent development of small ownerships, both among whites and blacks.   In the latter part of this chapter the rise of the share system and the beginning of independent renting will be treated.

As has already been pointed out, scarcity of laborers willing to work for wages was one of the controlling factors in the failure of the plantation regime.   This dearth of labor was due partly to migration, but also to the fact that there was an abundance of cheap land which former day laborers might acquire either as owners or renters.

There was no public land in Georgia in 1865.   The last land of this character had been distributed to citizens on the expulsion of the Cherokee Indians in the thirties.   This is a fact of some importance, as the existence of free public lands in Alabama, Mississippi, Louisiana, and Arkansas attracted many of the more energetic Georgians; while the demand for labor at higher prices in the West was drawing off thousands of negro laborers.

But of private land for sale there was plenty.   Of the total acreage of the state, 37,700,000, only 23,647,941 acres were reported in 1870[1] as being in farms, or 62.7 per cent., and only 18.1

---

[1] United States Census, 1870, *Industry and Wealth*, p. 120.

per cent. of the total acreage was classed as improved. That large section of south central and southeast Georgia known as the "Wiregrass country" had formerly been regarded as unsuited to agriculture, but the great demand for cotton, coincident with a remarkable development in the use of commercial fertilizers, brought this region into cultivation in the years following the war. Not only was this huge supply of land opened up, but there were also available many thousands of acres of improved lands in the older sections, now coming on the market with the breakup of plantations. A further supply of land was the "old field" or formerly cultivated land, abandoned in the exploitative processes characteristic of the ante-bellum period.[2]

One of the newspapers of the black belt in the years 1865 to 1872 was full of advertisements of land for sale. One issue in 1866[3] contained sixty-eight separate advertisements of lands for sale, aggregating 23,000 acres. These advertisements were rarely made by individuals or land companies, but generally gave notice of sales by officers of the law. They fall into three classes: sales to effect division of estates between heirs of deceased owners, sheriffs' sales to satisfy tax *fi fas,* and sales to satisfy judgments of creditors. Prices were not given, since sales were to be at public outcry. In running through the files of the newspaper referred to only two instances were found in which the price of lands actually sold was mentioned. In one instance, 400 acres in Appling County were sold at ten cents per acre, and in the other, two entire tracts of 400 acres in Montgomery county and 200 acres in Decatur county were sold for the lump sum of $2.50.[4] This land was considered mere waste. Indeed, it was many years before lands in two of these counties, Appling and Montgomery, could be sold at anything above a nominal price.

---

[2] *Southern Cultivator,* July, 1865. "We have never taken a railroad trip of fifty miles or more through Georgia or any of the adjoining states without being painfully impressed by the vast quantity of land lying everywhere, waste, unappropriated, and seemingly worthless. A great portion of the soil to which we allude, is known as "old field" or "wornout" land. It has been at one time in cultivation, and is now partially grown up in scrub pine, dwarf oak, broom-sedge, blackberry bushes, persimmon, etc., etc."

[3] Milledgeville [Ga.] *Southern Recorder,* Nov. 6, 1866.

[4] *Ibid,* Jan. 12, 1869.

The Comptroller-General's *Report*[5] for 1868–69 showed that the 30,816,025 acres returned for taxation were valued on the average at $2.82 per acre, but as these returns were made by the landowners themselves for purposes of taxation at a time when land taxes were high, they do not afford a trustworthy basis for a correct estimate as to land values.

Reliable data as to prices are, in fact, extremely scarce. In the general depression at the close of the war, the feeling was that values were low. One often meets such statements as this: "Before the War lands in Middle Georgia averaged perhaps ten dollars per acre, but now would not command half that price."[6] Similarly, lands in Southwest Georgia before the War were said to have ranged in price from twenty to thirty dollars, while after 1865 not more than five dollars could be realized on them. On the other hand, one would naturally expect that during the period of extraordinarily high prices of cotton, lands would be held at a high figure. The New York *Herald* was quoted[7] in 1869 to the effect that cotton land in Georgia had increased from fifty to three hundred per cent. in price since 1865, on account of the sudden revival of the cotton industry, and the most detailed information available tends, in a measure, to bear out this assertion. The United States Treasury Department published, in 1872, for the guidance of immigrants, a handbook[8] con-

---

[5] Georgia Comptroller General, *Report,* 1868–69, Table C.

[6] U. S. Department of Agriculture, *Yearbook,* 1866, pp. 570, 572.

[7] *Southern Recorder,* March 2, 1869.

[8] Young, Edward, Chief of Bureau of Statistics, Treasury Department, *Special Report on Immigration,* 1872. The following information was given with reference to improved farm lands in Georgia, the report covering forty-four counties.

Chatham County: Land held in large parcels; owners unwilling to divide; not more than one-fourth of the land cleared.

Glynn: Cotton lands $3 to $5 per acre; rice lands $40 to $50; good buildings.

Thomas: Lands to be had at from $5 to $10; about two-fifths under cultivation.

Spalding: Farms of about 200 acres available, one-half under cultivation; great want of improvements.

Decatur: $2 to $10, buildings indifferent, fences bad.

Dougherty, Lee, Baker: $15 to $20; one-third to one-half cultivated; log houses.

Muscogee: $5 to $15; log houses, piney woods, generally poor.

Terrell, Calhoun, Clay, Early: $5 to $8, good cabins.

Upson, Talbot, Harris: $6 to $30, three-fourths cultivated; buildings vary from log cabins to comfortable frame houses.

taining lists and prices of lands for sale in the several states. The information was obtained by correspondence with well-informed men in every locality, and, as the purpose of the publication was to attract immigration, it is unlikely that prices were exaggerated. The lands offered in Georgia ranged from $1.00 per acre in the Wiregrass country to $100 in the neighborhood of cities. The general level of the price quotations was higher than would be expected in view of the unsettled labor conditions and the rapidly falling price of cotton. Nearly all of the forty-four counties for which data were given in this Treasury publication lay in the Black Belt. The highest prices are found in the oldest part of the belt. In the newer southwestern section, where the land was more fertile, but was uncleared, for instance, in Terrell, Randolph, Calhoun, Early, and Decatur Counties, the prices were relatively low. These low prices were one cause of the movement of population in that direction. The prices were for "improved" farms, and, though the term was very loosely applied, as is shown by the descriptions, the land was probably in a cultivable condition. Unimproved lands in all these counties could be had at much lower prices, and it was doubtless out of these unimproved areas that most of the new farms presently to be mentioned were carved.

The sudden growth reported by the census in the number of farms and the decrease in the average size of farms in the

---

Randolph : $2 to $8, very inferior buildings.

Sumter, Webster, Dooly : $5 to $15.

Newton : $6 to $15 ; good land with ordinary improvements, $8 to $10.

Morgan and Putnam : $12 to $20, poor improvements.

Richmond, Burke and Screven, near Augusta : $25 to $100; at distance from the city, $2 to $15.

Wilkes, Taliaferro : large farms, owners unwilling to divide, improvements inferior.

Floyd, Walker, Chattooga, Polk : $8 to $15.

Clarke : $10 to $12 ; log buildings.

Cobb : $6.

Lincoln, Columbia, Elbert : $6.

Warren : $15 to $20, nearly all fenced and cultivated.

Troup : $5 to $50, one-half cultivated ; common buildings.

Fulton, DeKalb, Gwinnett : $10 to $25, one-fourth fenced.

Whitfield : $3 to $10, one-fourth cultivated ; log houses.

Pierce : $1 to $2 ; log houses.

South have justly been regarded as among the most conspicuous results of the Civil War. The change was immediate and far-reaching in Georgia. The following table indicates the extent to which the movement had progressed by 1880.[9]

Year.	Total farms.	Average size.	Total acres in farms.
1850..................	51,759	441	22,821,379
1860..................	62,003	430	26,650,490
1870..................	69,956	338	23,647,941
1880..................	138,626	188	26,043,282

The Census of 1870 was so defective as to be of little value in tracing the changes in the agricultural situation in the South in the decade after 1860. This unreliability is indicated by the fact that, whereas the number of farms in Georgia increased 10,244 between 1850 and 1860, a period when the tendency was for plantations to grow in size by absorbing small farms, there was between 1860 and 1870 an increase of only 8,000 farms, despite the fact that small ownership and tenancy were growing more rapidly than had ever before been the case. The corrective comes in the Census of 1880, which showed an enormous increase in the number of farms and a sharp decline in the average size of the holdings. It can scarcely be doubted that part of the change revealed in 1880 actually occurred between 1860 and 1870, but did not appear in 1870 because of the fact that the disturbed condition of affairs in the South made an accurate Census enumeration impossible. It is preferable, therefore, to use the Censuses of 1860 and 1880 for purposes of comparison. In the face of a decline of 600,000 acres under cultivation, the number of farms increased more than 100 per cent., while there was a decline in the average size of holdings from 430 to 188 acres. These facts indicate the partial failure of the plantation system and the development of small ownership and of tenancy.

---

[9] U. S. Census, 1900, V, *Agriculture,* pp. 688-692.

A classification of farms by size groups in 1860 and 1870 throws further light on the movement.[10]

	Acres 20–50	50–100	100–500	500–1,000	1,000+
1860.....	13,644	14,490	18,821	2,692	902
1870.....	21,971	18,371	17,490	1,506	419

Half of the farms of more than five hundred acres in size disappeared in ten years. The entire increase in farms is found in those of from twenty to one hundred acres.

No certain light can be thrown on the question to what extent this increase in the number of farms meant the spread of small ownership, on the one hand, and of tenancy, on the other. The United States Census published no statistics on land tenure until 1880. In that report (and the subsequent practice has been the same) the aggregate number of farms was given, followed by a classification into three groups, namely, farms operated by owners, farms operated by cash tenants, and farms operated by share tenants. Since, on the one hand, a single owner may operate several distinct farms, and, on the other, many landowners do not farm at all, it is obvious that the number of farms operated by owners does not by any means represent the number of landowners.

The only study of the spread of landownership that has been made in Georgia was the partial one by Banks in his *Economics of Land Tenure in Georgia.* Selecting from the 137 counties 31 which he regarded as typical, Mr. Banks examined in detail the original tax digests in the Comptroller General's office for the years 1873, 1880, 1890, and 1902; and for the year 1903 he counted the landowners in all of the counties.[11] He gave the number of white and colored owners separately for each of the five periods. In the case of the whites, these statistics went to show that there had been a 56 per cent. increase in the number

---

[10] U. S. Census, 1870, *Industry and Wealth,* p. 340. It is probable that a good many of the larger farms were not enumerated in 1870.
[11] Banks, *op. cit.,* app., pp. 119–134.

of white landowners from 1873 to 1902, and a decrease of 31 per cent. in the average size of the proprietorships.[12] The greatest rate of increase was between 1870 and 1880.

In the case of negroes, the Comptroller General has published each year since 1873 the total acreage owned by members of that race. The following table shows the negro-owned acreage for 1874 and for the subsequent decennial periods, beginning with 1880:[13]

1874	338,769 acres.
1880	586,664 "
1890	967,234 "
1900	1,075,073 "

Banks worked out the average size of negro holdings for the thirty-one counties considered by him at the years 1873, 1880, 1890, and 1902, with the following result:[14]

1873	113.9 acres.
1880	98.3 "
1890	71.0 "
1902	64.3 "

On the assumption that the average size of negro-owned farms for the thirty-one counties roughly represents the average for the entire state, the approximate number of negro landowners for the above years is as follows:

Year.	Total acreage.	Number landowners.
1874	338,769	2,974
1880	586,664	5,968
1890	927,234	13,623
1900	1,075,073	16,719
1903	1,246,455	18,715

The figures for 1903 are the latest that can be given. They make a very poor showing for the negro as a landowner in

[12] *Ibid*, p. 35.
[13] DuBois, *Negro Landowner of Georgia*, p. 665.
[14] Banks, app., pp. 112, 127–130.

Georgia. While they composed, in 1900, 46.7 per cent. of the
population of the state, they had taxable titles to only one
twenty-fifth of the land.

The progress of the negroes in acquiring land did not seem
at all satisfactory to their contemporary leaders. A conference
of social settlement workers in Georgia and the South met in
Atlanta in 1875, and went on record as follows:[15]

> "The outlook is not encouraging. Many of the negroes are making
> a noble and successful struggle against all their difficulties, without
> and within, but as a rule they are not acquiring homes and property,
> their enthusiasm for education is yielding to the chilling influence of
> their poverty, and their innate evil propensities, uncorrected by their
> sensational religion, are dragging them downward. Numbers are be-
> coming discouraged as to acquiring property."

Further evidence that the development of small proprietorship
among negroes was not striking may be found in the detailed
investigation conducted by the Bureau of the Census in 1880.[16]
The replies from Georgia may be summarized as follows:

In Northwest Georgia, five counties reported that not more
than one negro farmer in twenty owned his land; two counties
reported one in ten, two reported one in four or five. In the
Piedmont region, twenty counties reported not more than one
in a hundred; five, about one in twenty-five; others one in ten.
Bibb County, containing the city of Macon, was reported as
having nine negro landowners out of ten farmers. In the Central Cotton Belt, thirteen counties reported not more than one
in a hundred, five about one in fifty, three one in twenty,
two one in five. In the Wiregrass section, seven counties reported "very few," seven one in ten or twenty, seven from one in
four to one in two. Appling and Mitchell Counties reported
"most of the negro laborers own land." Thomas County reported "the number is large and increases."

Banks's study showed that, while there had been a large absolute increase in the number of white landowners, "the owners
stood [in 1900] in about the same numerical relation to the

---

[15] DuBois, *op. cit.*, p. 666, quoting from *American Missionary*, June, 1875.
[16] U. S. Census, 1880, VI, *Cotton Production*, Pt. 2, p. 174.

total white population as in 1860,'' that is to say, about every other white family in the state owned land.[17] One is led, then, to suspect that the growth of small ownerships was not so widespread as has usually been supposed. By far the larger part of the increase in number of farms in the post-bellum period represents increase of tenant farmers. By 1880, 44.8 per cent. of all the farms in the state were tenant farms.

This growth of tenancy meant a weakening of control over agricultural operations on the part of the former managing class. The readjustment of the labor system in Georgia has been a process of decentralization, from complete control by employers of wage gangs to the regime of independent renters. An account of this process has been preserved for one of the large Oglethorpe County plantations.[18] For several years following emancipation, the force of laborers was divided into two squads, the arrangement and method of work being as in the ante-bellum period. Each squad was under an overseer, or foreman. The hands were given a share of the crop. As time went on, the control of the foreman became irksome to the negroes. As a consequence the squads were split up into smaller and smaller groups, still working for a part of the crop, and still using the owner's teams. This process of disintegration continued until each laborer worked separately, without any oversight. The change involved great trouble and loss. Mules were ill-treated, the crop was badly worked and often the tenant stole the landlord's share. It became necessary to abandon the sharing feature. The owner sold his mules to the tenants, thereby putting on them the burden of loss incidental to careless handling of stock. It became impracticable to keep the cabins grouped when each man worked on a separate farm, since some of the farms were at a distance from the "quarters." New cottages were, therefore, built scatteringly in convenient places near springs. The negroes now planted what they pleased, and worked when they liked, the landlord interfering only to require that enough cotton be planted to pay the rent. The

---

[17] Banks, p. 43.
[18] Barrow, D. C., in *Scribner's Magazine*, April, 1881.

author of the sketch of this plantation said: ''The slight supervision which is exercised over these tenants [in 1880] may surprise those ignorant of how completely the relations between the races at the South have changed.''

It is to be noted that in this instance the share arrangement was adopted from the first. Had wages been paid for a year or two and then the change to shares been made, the case would have been typical of the history of the decentralization of agricultural operations in Georgia.

Another Oglethorpe County farmer states[19] that ''As a general thing we first employed some hands for standing wages and some for part of the crop. We worked them all together, supervised them and gave each one his part in Fall of the year. The renting system, beginning in 1875, has gradually gained until now one half of the tenants or more are renters.'' He attributed the growth of renting to the unwillingness of the negroes to work in gangs under supervision. It is to be noted that he worked wage hands and share tenants together, under supervision.

Questions 4 and 5 of the inquiry designated as ''Inquiries I'' asked whether, in case the wage system had been used in 1865, it was subsequently abandoned, and what substitute was made. In every such case the share system had been so substituted, the time of the change varying from 1867 to 1886. Several replies indicated that the substitution was only partial, both wage and share laborers being employed. The reasons for the change will appear from the following quotations: Bartow County: ''Hired labor became too sorry and unreliable, because, as now, it was so scarce.'' Jefferson County: ''It was more profitable and less risk to engage part of the labor for wages, part on the share system and part tenants.'' Muscogee County: ''The negro first became a cropper on shares as a step towards what you call in your inquiry 'a more independent' position. Also largely due to the fact that if he hired himself out for wages he alone drew wages and his family such pay for day work as

---

[19] *Inquiries I*, letter of C. A. Stevens, January, 1912.

they might secure on the farm. By running the crop himself
he could put his wife and children in his own crop.'' Baldwin
County: ''It became difficult to employ wages labor.''

The rapidity with which the share system was adopted is indicated by the statement in the Freedman's Bureau report of
1868 [20] that most of the contracts for that year were for a part
of the crop. This was an exaggeration, but it shows that there
was a wholesale abandonment of the wage system. The extent
to which the movement had progressed was first definitely
known in 1880, when the Census showed that 31.4 per cent.
of all Georgia farms were operated on the share arrangement.

For a number of years after the introduction of this system
of crop-sharing, there was no uniformity of practice as to what
share should be given to the laborer. The share varied with
the relative bargaining power of the parties, with variations
in the fertility of the soil, and with the amount and character
of the equipment furnished by the employer. At the present
time in the Black Belt one rarely meets with any other basis
of division than the half. Outside of that region, in sections
where tenants are largely white, a ''third-and-fourth'' system is
practiced.

When the system of sharing first came into vogue, the laborer's share was low, but scarcity of labor and the influence of
the Freedmen's Bureau increased his share.[21] A bureau in-
spector drove through the country from Thomas to Dougherty
County, in 1866, visiting plantations on the way. He reported[22] that contracts for the year 1865 had ranged from one-
sixth to one-tenth of the crop to the laborer. The Treasury
Department investigation of 1869–70 showed great diversity
of practice in the forty-four counties considered,[23] but the half
was the most frequent share, in cases where the laborer fed
himself. Nearly all of the replies to the question on this point
in ''Inquiries I'' were to the effect that the half was the share
given the tenant, Hancock County furnishing the single excep-

---

[20] 40 Cong., 3 sess., *House Ex. Docs.*, 3, No. I, p. 1044.
[21] 39 Cong., 1 sess., *Sen. Ex. Docs.*, II, 88–89.
[22] *Ibid*, p. 91.
[23] Young, *Report on Immigration*, 1872, p. 133.

tion. The United States Department of Agriculture in the report of 1876[24] stated that "Four-fifths of the counties of Georgia report one-half for labor subsisting itself." This report was based on evidence collected in every county in the state and may be accepted as authoritative. Curiously enough, the report also said that two-thirds of all the farms of Georgia were operated on the share system, whereas the Census report four years later showed that a few less than one-third of the farms were operated on that basis.

Of first importance in connection with the development of tenancy is the matter of supervision or control of labor. If the planter continued to work the share tenants in groups under strict supervision by himself or his representative, the plantation organization was not seriously impaired. Neither could the plantation be said to have disappeared when the tenants were given separate farms, provided the owner supervised their farming. But if the laborers were scattered over a large plantation and were allowed to escape from all control, the former organization cannot be said to have remained intact. The plantation, in fact, in such cases, became a collection of little farms, independently operated. At the present time, an unsupervised "cropper," as share tenants have come to be known, is almost never met with. The supervision of his operations is as close as the planter can make it, the right of control being based on the fact that the owner furnishes all the capital necessary to make the crop. Few men would now think of entrusting such capital to uncontrolled negroes, and such evidence as is to be found tends to show that this practice of supervision dates back to the inception of the share system. In "Inquiries I," the question was asked: "Did you closely supervise share tenants (immediately after 1865)?" Some of the replies may be given. Oglethorpe County: "I closely attended to all the details of the crop and managing the hands, was obliged to. No measure of success could be attained any other way." Putnam County: "I gave better attention

[24] U. S. Department of Agriculture, *Yearbook*, 1876, p. 131.

than now, as we worked old slaves then. Now we have the new generation which is worthless." Baldwin: "I gave close supervision." Another from Baldwin: "Personal and close supervision." Jefferson County: "I did supervise the share hands, as my interest was dependent on good crops made by them." Bulloch County: "Were supervised more closely than renters, because I had more at stake." Hancock County: "I closely supervised."

Three of the replies may be taken to mean that share tenants were unsupervised. Gordon County: "They generally wanted to farm independent of us and mostly have made sorry crops." Bartow County: "About the same" (as renters.) Gwinnett County: "Yes, they are independent, then and now." These three counties are in North Georgia outside of the Black Belt. Question 2 of the inquiry asked for the number and color of the laborers. The Gordon County farmer had four whites and one negro; the Bartow County correspondent employed seven whites, no negroes; the Gwinnett County farmer had two whites and three blacks. All of the letters to the effect that the share tenants were supervised came, with one exception, from the Black Belt. Those planters who supervised share tenants were large employers of almost exclusively black labor. The Oglethorpe planter quoted employed one white and twenty-five blacks; the Wilkes County letter came from an employer of twenty-five to thirty negroes; the Putnam County planter worked twenty-seven negroes; the Baldwin County correspondent one white, and forty blacks, the Jefferson County planter, one hundred and twenty negroes.

This evidence is too slender for a generalization, but it suggests that in the black belt share croppers were strictly supervised, while outside the belt, many white croppers were not subjected to control.

There were, on the other hand, planters who tried the plan of unsupervised share tenancy. The Barrow plantation[25] is a case in point. Maltreatment of animals and loss of crops resulted, and the system was abandoned for renting. The Agri-

---

[25] See *Ante*, p. 45.

cultural Department correspondent for Georgia said in 1876[26]:
"Many farmers [of Georgia] have been nearly ruined by neglect to exercise wholesome supervision of the farm economy,
and waste and improvidence of share croppers. Some have
benefitted themselves and laborers by a judicious control." Similarly, in 1880, the following note occurs in a census publication[27]:

"The plan of dividing crops under the share system is an equitable
one, and if it were properly carried out there could be no cause of complaint, but the owner, in nine cases out of ten, has not only to furnish
his farm, but to supply all the needs of the tenant, without having any
control over the time or acts of the tenant, who is often seen idling
and loitering when his crop requires his immediate attention. Tenants
owe the owners for provisions, clothing, tobacco, etc., and in many
cases they are indifferent as to whether they produce enough to pay
the owners these advances made during the season. Thus the landlords annually lose largely by this system of shares, simply because
they have all the risks and no corresponding control."

A Burke County planter writing to *The Cultivator* in 1868
relates practically the same experience.[28] His operations failed
in 1865 and 1866 largely on account of the bad seasons. In
1867, using the wage system, he made almost enough to recoup
the losses of the two former years and pay expenses of 1867;
in 1868 he changed over to the unsupervised share system, and
even as early as May he saw from the attitude of the laborers
and the condition of their fields that the experiment would be
a failure. His opinion was that "Negroes left to their own judgment, and their own volition must fail, for with a very few exceptions they have neither, and where you work on shares, they are
beyond cavil co-partners, and they have a right, and in the full-
ness of their conceit, exercise that right, to have a say-so in everything." The most instructive instance of the disastrous conse-
quences likely to follow from allowing share tenants to farm without supervision was furnished by Mr. David Dickson, who was for
many years regarded as one of the ablest Georgia planters. In

---

[26] U. S. Department of Agriculture, *Yearbook*, 1876, p. 132.
[27] U. S. Census, 1880, VI, *Cotton Production*, Pt. 2, p. 172. Letter from a
Georgia correspondent.
[28] *Southern Cultivator*, May, 1868.

spite of large experience and ample capital, Mr. Dickson found himself unable to make a profit with cotton at a high price.[29]

It seems clear from the evidence that unsupervised share farming was a failure; but it was impossible to impose restrictions on negroes who had been permitted to work on this system. The solution of the problem lay in a more complete separation of landlord and tenant, in other words, in real tenancy or renting.

The practice of renting lands arose from a variety of causes. Many planters in the unsettled condition of labor did not care

---

[29] *Ibid,* February, 1869. This communication, written by a special correspondent of the Cincinnati *Commercial,* dated Augusta, Ga., April 11, 1868, was reprinted by the *Cultivator.*

"Mr. Dickson's experience in planting is, of course, valuable chiefly to southern planters. A general adoption of his method of cultivation would more than double the products of the country and the profits of the farmer. But his experience with the freedmen will be more interesting to Northern men. It is especially valuable because it is trustworthy. There is no guesswork in it, for his accounts of labor and produce have been accurately kept both before and since the war. He hires his hands for a share of the crop, giving the choice of three different contracts. By one they pay for their rations and are given one-third of the crop, by another the freedmen obtain only the land from the employer and pay all expenses, furnishing their own stock and tools, these give one-third of the crop for the rent of the land. By the third, the laborer and employer share the expenses and the crops equally, in all cases the use of the land being considered a fair offset to the work of the laborer. *The men work in companies of from six to ten.* Each of these companies has a certain amount of land alloted to it, and it receives the share of the crop grown on that field. *No overseers are employed, and except that the manner of cultivation is prescribed by Mr. Dickson, they work about as they please.* Now for the results. In 1861, Mr. Dickson paid $13,000 for manures, worked sixty hands, and made 850 bales of cotton. In 1867, as good a season for crops, he worked one hundred and forty hands, paid $13,000 for manures, and made seven hundred bales of cotton, fifty of which wasted in the field because it was not picked out in time. Heretofore his loss of stock has amounted to $2,000 yearly. Last year the animals which died or were killed were worth $10,000. The freedmen use the mule very severely, beating them unmercifully and the loss so entailed is no inconsiderable item of the planter's expenses. With slaves Mr. Dickson produced from ten to fifteen bales of cotton to the hand. With freedmen he made three bales to the hand in 1866 (a bad season) and five and a half bales in 1867. Before the war from eight hundred to twelve hundred pounds of pork were made to each hand. Now the stock of hogs is nearly annihilated, and profits from this source are cut off. A large fortune was made before the war raising cotton at eight or nine cents a pound. At thirty cents a pound the crop of 1866 entailed a loss of several thousand dollars, and in 1867 fifteen cents a pound barely paid expenses, here where cotton is raised more cheaply, perhaps, than on any other farm in the south. Such decided proof of the demoralization of the laborers I have nowhere else found, because elsewhere the results were rather guessed at than deduced from accurate data."

The significant words have been italicised.

to attempt farming, and, unable to realize on their holdings, or unwilling to sell, turned over their lands to white and black renters, who, under the lien laws, could get their supplies from merchants, sometimes with, sometimes without, the landlord's endorsement. Other planters, owning large bodies of land and desiring to continue operations, were able to secure a sufficient force of laborers to man only part of the plantation, and therefore rented the balance, rather than have it remain idle. Yet other planters, influenced by the new impulse towards popular education, moved to the towns to educate their children, and under such circumstances rented their lands, the only alternative to selling, since the wage or share system was impractical without constant oversight. But the most potent factor in bringing about the renting system was the negroes' desire for complete emancipation from control.[30] By reason of the scarcity of labor they were able to realize their wishes. When the movement was once begun, it grew with great rapidity, for as soon as the negroes who were working as day laborers or share hands saw the large degree of personal liberty enjoyed by those who had succeeded in attaining the position of renters, they speedily demanded like privileges, and, in a large number of cases, the planters were not in a position to refuse.

The workings of the share and renting systems will be discussed in the following chapter. The essential differences between the two systems may be briefly explained at this point. Under the renting system the landlord furnishes only the land and house. All supplies are furnished by the tenant. The landlord has nothing to do with the tenant's crop, no right of supervision as to the sort of crops grown or the amount of labor expended. The rental under this arrangement is commonly stated

---

[30] Industrial Commission, *Report,* X, p. 487. Testimony of F. M. Norfleet: "This disposition to rent that the negro has chiefly in this country is due to a desire to have charge of his own affairs, without being hindered. That being the most pleasant arrangement for him, is the one he insists on in making his arrangements for the year with his landlord. The landlord himself would prefer the share system. It is the best because then the negroes operate under his supervision and the farm as a rule is kept up better, but on account of the scarcity of labor the landlords through this section of the country have to pursue largely whatever plan suits the labor best."

in terms of cotton, though outside of the Black Belt there is a considerable amount of cash renting.

Under the share system, the landlord supplies everything necessary to make the crop, except the manual labor, and the owner and tenant are in a sense co-partners in the undertaking. Since the landlord has undertaken all the risk, he claims the right of complete control over the tenant and the crop, just as in the case of a day laborer. It is this supervision that the darkies resent. It is a well-established fact that their profits under the supervised share system are usually far higher than they can make as independent renters. Profit, however, is a secondary consideration. In 1880 more than twenty per cent. of all the Black Belt farms were being operated on a renting basis, by far the larger part of the renters being negroes.

Question 8 of "Inquiries I" was: "Did you later abandon the share arrangement for a renting system; if so, when and why." Only four negative replies were received. Three of these were from counties outside the Black Belt and the fourth was a border county. All of the four employed some white labor, two of them a majority of whites. Two of the four were among those outside the Black Belt who had exercised no supervision over share farmers—apparently no demand for a change where there was no supervision. All of the planters who had closely supervised their laborers under the share system later adopted renting. The following are some of the reasons given for the change in Black Belt counties.

Oglethorpe County: "The negro became less willing to work in large bodies on the large plantations, they became harder to manage and many negroes began to desire to get off to themselves and run one and two horse farms. The large landowners finding that they could no longer get the negro low or cheap enough to allow a margin of profit, began to place their tenant houses all over their farms and rent to their tenants." Wilkes County: "A large part of those renting only wanted more liberty to do as they felt like and not to improve their condition." Baldwin County: "The change was gradual. As the new negro came on, it required an overseer to every plow to get any work done, as the share laborer got his supplies, he would not work, as he had all he desired. The rental seemed best as more responsibility was on the tenant." Another from Putnam: "Can't control any system, but seek a good hand for wage, as cropper or tenant. The negro practically decides the system applied to farming. The negro naturally seeks the position as laborer affording the most absence of white supervision—the privilege of personal independence." Muscogee County: "In their effort to gain a still more independent position, they began demanding rent privileges where they could enforce it." Hancock County: "Because I moved family to town to educate children, and practically abandoned plantation to renters. Still retained some share hands and gave to them what attention I could, didn't work well to have both on same place, and had to drop share plan."

Before 1880 all the forces which determined the post-bellum history of agricultural labor in Georgia were in operation. The decline of the plantation organization and the rise of the two dominant types of tenancy have been traced as far as it has been found possible in the absence of comprehensive statistical data. After 1880 the decennial publications of the Census Bureau make it possible to study the movement with more definite results.

CHAPTER IV

THE CONTRASTING TYPES OF TENANCY IN THE NEW REGIME: CROPPING AND RENTING

In confining the remainder of this monograph to a study of tenancy in Georgia two considerations are controlling. The first is that the growth of tenancy has been the most striking development in the post-bellum period; the other, that no data is available for a statistical study of the modern plantation. Under the classification followed by the Bureau of the Census, the plantation as an economic unit is ignored. This is unfortunate, not only because the plantation is by no means a negligible factor in present-day Southern agriculture, but also for the further reason that confusion unavoidably follows the Census practice of classifying as farms the holdings of share tenants. While, therefore, the development in the plantation system cannot be traced except inferentially from the movements in tenancy, the plantation lends itself readily to description in individual cases, and a detailed account of at least one plantation will be given.

An effort was made at the 1910 Census to obtain information bearing on the modern plantation system. In addition to the regular farm schedules, a Plantation Schedule was distributed among the enumerators, and a large number of these were filled and returned to the Bureau. Supplementary data was collected by special agents in the summer of 1911, but no publication of these results has so far been made. The present writer was one of the special agents and was assigned to the state of Georgia. The plan of the investigation was as follows: The state was divided into ten districts. Each district was marked out so as to include counties similar in their general characteristics. A special schedule of inquiries was prepared, designed to cover every feature of plantation life. Questions were asked to elicit information as to the size of the plantation and amount of investment, character of equipment, method of farming, type of labor employed, method of organizing the labor into an industrial unit, method of supervising labor, relative efficiency of wage laborers, share tenants and renters, the general condition of the laboring population, financially, morally, educationally. In every district the agent obtained by filling out these schedules a detailed description of a number of plantations in actual operation. When not engaged in obtaining answers to schedule questions, merchants, bankers, farmers, tenants, and laborers were consulted as to the general conditions of plantation life. On the conclusion of work in a given district, a "District Report" was made, following a scheme prepared by Bureau officials and men familiar with the subject. Three months were spent in this work and a large amount of fresh material was gathered bearing on the present situation in the plantation belt. Copies of plantation schedules and district reports were retained by the agent, and these, with other materials to be mentioned, form the basis of this and the succeeding chapters.[1]

Another body of unpublished and hitherto unused material are letters received in reply to a questionnaire prepared in 1902 by the Division of Statistics of the United States Department of Agriculture.[2] This was an inquiry into the tenant system in the country at large. From Georgia one hundred and forty-one replies were received, representing eighty-two counties.

In addition to the above, valuable information has been obtained from the replies to an inquiry conducted in 1906 by the Department of Rural Economics in the University of Wisconsin.[3] Though only twenty-two replies were received from Georgia, the letters are of unusual value.

---

[1] See Bibliographical Note, *post,* pp. 115–116. The descriptions of individual plantations will be designated as "Plantation Schedules, 1911," and the district reports as "Reports on Georgia Plantation Districts, 1911."

[2] See Bibliographical Note, *post,* p. 116. This material is cited as *"Inquiries II, 1902."*

[3] See Bibliographical Note, *post,* p. 116. This material is referred to as *"Inquiries III, 1906."*

The following table shows the status of the various classes of farmers at the four Census periods for which such data has been collected.[4]

	1880	1890	1900	1910
Total farms..............	138,626	171,071	224,691	291,211
Owners....................	76,451 (55.1)	79,477 (46.4)	81,603 (40.1)	100,231 (34.6)
Cash tenants..............	18,557 (13.4)	29,413 (17.2)	58,750 (26.2)	82,387 (28.2)
Share tenants.............	43,618 (31.5)	62,181 (36.4)	75,810 (33.7)	108,593 (37.2)

When this data comes to be rearranged by races and sections of the state, the figures will be more suggestive. However, certain well-defined and constant movements are revealed by the data in the above form. In the first place, there has been a regular and large increase in the total number of farms throughout the period, the increase being more rapid than the growth of population. This increase is due principally to the steady disintegration of large plantations, a movement which is still going ahead with unabated vigor. This disintegration has been in part a real, in part only a nominal division. A second cause of the increase has been the bringing into cultivation of new land in South Georgia with the gradual disappearance of the pine forests.[5]

The percentage of farms operated by owners has declined from 55.1 per cent. in 1880 to 34.6 per cent. in 1910. This fact has been misunderstood in Georgia, wide currency having been given

---

[4] U. S. Census, *Agriculture*, 1880, 1890, 1900, 1910. The term "Owners" is an abbreviation of "Farms operated by owners." In this class are included part owners, owners and tenants, and managers, the sub-classes being too small to affect the percentages. The data for 1910 was supplied by the Agricultural Division of the Census Bureau in advance of publication. In the final revision slight changes may occur. In parenthesis is given the percentage which each class of farmers formed of the total number of farmers at the given census period. For a similar table for white and black farmers separately, see *post*, p. 123.

[5] *Plantation Schedules*, 1911, No. 20. The holding described in this schedule illustrates the way in which turpentine forests are being transformed into farms. The place, which can scarcely be called a "plantation," is a tract of 7,000 acres, of which only 900 are in cultivation. The report states that the principal interest of the owner is the lumber and turpentine business. Farming is only incidental. The owner expects eventually to become a planter on a large scale and as fast as land is cut over he rents it to tenants under an arrangement by which clearing the land of stumps offsets the rent.

to the idea that it has meant the growth of tenancy at the expense of owner-operated farms.   This, however, has not been the case. Throughout the period there has been a steady and healthy increase in the absolute number of farms operated by owners; certainly the increase of farms in this catagory during the last decade affords small ground for uneasiness.   The period from 1890 to 1900 was one in which agricultural depression reached its nadir, cotton falling below five cents.   This depression was not only severe but was continuous over a longer period than any other in the history of the country.   That there should have been an increase of more than two thousand farms worked by owners during that decade is remarkable.   With returning prosperity in 1900, landownership received a striking impetus, as is indicated by the twenty thousand increase in farms operated by owners in the last decade.   Small ownership has been steadily growing, not declining, during the four decades since the Civil War.   The spread of tenancy has not involved a decline of owners.   For instance, suppose that on a given farm twenty hired laborers were employed.   The Census would record this unit as one farm. Now, if by the time the Census enumerators visited that farm again, the twenty laborers had become share tenants, using the same land and working as formerly under the eye of the owner, the essential economic unity of the plantation having remained unimpaired, the farm would be reported not as one operated by the owner, but as twenty operated by share tenants.   Clearly there is a fallacy in supposing that such a change as this has in any way affected the number of farms operated by owners.   It is to be remembered that the large majority of tenants are just such share tenants.

Fifty per cent. of the white farmers in the state own their farms.   The percentage of farmers working their own land is lowered by reason of the small percentage of negro farmers who own their land, and in the view of the writer it would be a social advantage if the number of negroes operating their own land was reduced and the less efficient class of negro owners should resume their former positions as day laborers.[6]

---

[6] Hoffman, F. L., *Race Traits and Tendencies of the American Negro.* In American Economics Association, *Publications,* XI, 1896.   A view similar to the

The growth of share tenant holdings represents a nominal or apparent increase in the number of farms. They should not be regarded as separate and distinct farms, since they are analogous to the squares on a checkerboard, the essential unity of which is not destroyed by the division. This point will receive further treatment presently. It will be observed from the table that while a majority of the tenant farms are share farms, this class of tenants has only succeeded in maintaining its relative position since 1880, while cash tenants have increased at a very rapid rate. Herein lies the only disquieting feature of the development. To the extent that these cash tenants are irresponsible negroes, without capital and intelligence, the growth of cash tenancy is a distinct evil. It is, on the other hand, an evidence of progress in the case of those efficient white and black men who are qualified for the higher economic position.

It is necessary at this point to draw a clear line of demarcation between the two forms of tenancy. Cash and share tenancy are found all over the United States, and the relative merits of the two systems have been discussed by all leading authorities on rural economics. Cash tenancy usually represents an economic advance over share tenancy. The common practice in the country at large is for the young man without capital but with a larger share of ambition and energy than is usually possessed by the day laborer to begin life as a share tenant. He incurs under this system little risk. The land and capital goods necessary for farming are supplied by the landlord, who actively manages the undertaking. The combination of self-interest on the part of the share tenant and the entrepreneurial efficiency of the landowner, usually an experienced farmer, form an excellent arrangement.[7] When the share tenant has accumulated sufficient

---

above as to negro landownership. "From personal observation I incline to agree with the writer who sees little benefit accruing from negro ownership of land. As a rule their "farms" are such in name only, and the cultivation of the soil and the condition of the grounds are of the lowest order."

[7] Taylor, H. C., *Agricultural Economics* (New York, 1911), p. 263. "Participation of the landlord in the management of the farm is the chief reason for the success of share tenancy in this country. This point has been emphasized over and over again in the communications received from men who are in a position to know. Share tenancy is, as a rule, more profitable to the landlord only when the farm is under his immediate supervision. If the management must be left entirely to the tenant farmer, the cash system is usually preferable to the landlord."

capital to stock a farm, and has acquired the skill and experience
necessary to successful farming, he strikes out for himself as an
independent renter. He is now in a much more advantageous
position, because after the payment of a fixed rental per acre, all
of the increment of product due to his superior managerial efficiency goes to himself, whereas the share farmer must pay pro-
portionally more rent as the product of his industry increases.[8]
More careful culture and more constant industry may normally
be expected of cash tenants. From the standpoint of social production, the cash system is preferable, because it makes for a more
perfect utilization of the land; indeed, one of the difficulties attaching to the cash system is the tendency of the farmer to force
the soil in the effort to extract from it the maximum yield during
a given tenancy.[9]

The same qualities being necessary for the cash tenant as for
the landowner, success as a cash tenant often means an easy
transition to landownership. Experience has shown that this
evolution may be expected.

The above considerations do not apply in the case of the negro
element of tenants in Georgia. In that state, share tenancy im-
plies close supervision on the part of the owner; cash tenancy,
freedom from such control. It has been well said that the passage of the negro from the former to the latter class "marks not
his greater ability but his greater opportunity to declare his independence from the close supervision of the landlord." It is
the escaping from supervision, not the larger opportunity of profits that the negro has in mind in shifting from the position of
wage earner or share tenant to renter. The history of the normal
negro agricultural laborer is about as follows. He begins as a
youth working for wages. As soon as he has a family that can be
utilized for field work he becomes a share tenant. Under the
semi-compulsion of this system, he makes good profits, and, if he
has any capacity for saving, can in a short time buy a mule and
a few tools, and set up as a renter. So great has been the competition for laborers and so completely have the negroes had the upper hand in this matter, that negro wage earners and share

---

[8] Carver, T. N., *Principles of Rural Economics* (Boston, 1911), p. 232.
[9] Taylor, *Agricultural Economics*, pp. 269–270. Carver, *Rural Economics*,
p. 232.

hands have in many instances been able to achieve an independent position even without the inconvenience of having to save the small amount necessary to stock a renter's farm. In thousands of cases where there was not the slightest reason to anticipate success from the venture, landlords have been forced to sell to negroes on credit tools and work animals or to rent the equipment along with the land, and to set up laborers as renters. Being, in the mass, of low grade efficiency, the cash tenant begins getting in debt the first year; after two or three years everything he has is taken for debt, and he returns to his former position of day laborer or share tenant.[10]

Sometimes the share tenant uses his profits to make an initial payment on a piece of land and becomes a small proprietor. His experience as a landowner is often similar to his experience as a renter.[11] He struggles on from year to year, making a miserable living, being able to exist solely because of his deplorably low

---

[10] *Plantation Schedules,* 1911, No. 19. The following extract from the report on a Brooks County plantation gives a typical case of negro experience as a renter. "Anthony Moore, a splendid worker, had a farm on this plantation, twenty acres in cotton and fifteen in corn, in 1905. He made thirteen bales of cotton and a large quantity of corn [working as a share tenant]. The attached original account [a sheet torn from the plantation ledger] shows the large amount of cash this negro got during the year, as well as other advances, and the credits of cotton, half the bale being credited in each case. He settled up the entire account and had corn and meat extra, not to mention the $100 in cash which he got just prior to the final settlement. This negro abandoned the place the following year, because the landlord would not rent to him, and he had enough to buy a mule. He rented a farm from Mr. ⸺, another Brooks County planter, and wound up his first year $70 in debt and nothing to show for the year's work. His former employer was interested to see how the case would turn out, as this was a good negro, so far as his application to work was concerned. The next year the deficit was taken up by another planter, named ⸺. At the end of that year, he was worse off than at the end of the former year. The negro came to Mr. ⸺, the original employer, last Sunday and told him of his troubles. Mr. ⸺ expects him to go back to work as a cropper, but has no doubt that as soon as he pays out of debt and saves enough to buy an animal he will again resort to renting. His observation is that after an unusually good crop year, it is very difficult to get labor for the following year. The negroes have all made money and do not want to work again as croppers, that is, practically day laborers receiving their pay at the end of the year."

[11] *Inquiries II,* 1902, Letter from Upson County: "The writer soon after the negroes were freed, undertook to aid many of his old family negroes, with disastrous results in all except one case. Will mention one case of late occurrence to illustrate. Fourteen years ago I bought a farm of 120 acres and a fine mule and wagon and other items of supplies for one of my favorite negroes, and sold them to him for what they all cost me. During that long time he has only paid the cost of the mule and wagon, and last year permitted the land to be sold for taxes, and I had to redeem same."

standard of life, using the least efficient stock and implements and the most antiquated methods of cultivation. It is little short of miraculous if he maintains himself, for it is a struggle against all the tendencies of the time. He is the marginal farmer, and with the increasing value of land that must follow a rapidly growing population, the likelihood of his surviving seems small.

There is an element of negroes who are prospering as renters and landowners. In the investigations of 1911, the writer made it a rule to ask every planter whether he knew of cases of success-ful negroes, and found no planter who could not mention by name such cases. These negroes are the hope of the race, because they are a standing refutation of the belief held by many persons that the negro is incapable of advancement. No claim is here made that negroes are not progressing. Such a claim would be idle in the face of the fact that in 1910 they were assessed for taxation in Georgia on $32,234,047 worth of property, including 1,607,970 acres of land.[12] The point on which insistence is made is that the mass of the race are wholly unfit for economic independence, and that they are sacrificing their best chance for well-being in seek-ing too rapid a divorcement from the tutelage in industry through which they should pass. The economic motive that urges men of other races to labor is weak in the negro race.[13] Any influences which would tend to increase his wants are to be welcomed. He needs larger desires and the pressure of competition for work. However slovenly his work under the conditions that have existed for nearly a half century, he is assured of a living, mean though it be, and this is sufficient. He feels no necessity for greater in-dustry, and hence will not work unless encouraged to do so by the presence of some supervisor.

In the preceding chapter it was shown that from the beginning of the share system some planters exercised supervision, and that those who did not became involved in failure. Gradually all

---

[12] Georgia Comptroller General, *Report*, 1910, Table 17.

[13] Hammond, *Cotton Industry*, p. 186. "The freedmen and their descendants are generally lacking in energy and ambition. They possess none of the quali-ties which are found in all progressive workers. Their labor succeeds only when it is subject to constant supervision . . . Poorer farming can scarcely be found than on the numerous plantations in the South where the absentee pro-prietor has rented out his land to the negro cropper and has left the latter free to conduct the farming in his own way."

share tenants who could be retained were placed under supervision and those who refused to acquiesce in the arrangement took the further step and became renters. In this way the landlord either recovered his manifest right to safeguard the property necessary to operate a share system, or, by renting out the land, tended to escape from responsibility as to the capital goods required.

Planters have been virtually unanimous during the entire postbellum period in resenting the growth of renting. They feel that where the laboring class is of such a low order, complete control should remain in the hands of the capitalist class. They know that skill, industry, knowledge, and frugality are essential to successful farming, and they know that negroes in general lack these qualities. The indictment against the renter is overwhelming. Of the twenty-two letters received in "Inquiries III," fourteen were emphatically in favor of the share system; five preferred renting because they wanted to get rid of the annoyance and trouble incidental to working with negro labor, and only one preferred renting because it is "less trouble and pays better." In the course of the summer's work of 1911, only two or three planters were found in Georgia who would speak a favorable word for renting. Of the entire number of plantation schedules obtained, in only one case was the owner in favor of renting, and it is significant that in that instance the renters were supervised in much the same way that share tenants are usually controlled.[14] Seventeen of the twenty-two planters from whom replies were received in "Inquiries III," in answer to a specific question, said that the most serious problem confronting the planter who rented his lands was the impoverishment and deterioration of the soil. One letter may be reproduced as the type of them all.

"The renter being independent, obligated for so much rent, is in ninety-nine cases out of a hundred, left to his own pleasure and judgment; the result of which is, the farm on which he works is consist-

---

[14] *Plantation Schedules*, 1911, No. 18. This was an interesting case. The planter operated about 2,500 acres of land, all in the hands of negro renters. These renters own their stock and tools. Some of them have been with the planter twenty-five years and all for long periods. They were carefully selected. The owner exercises close supervision over them in an advisory way, visiting each place once a week. He believes this supervision to be "absolutely necessary." His renters are very willing to work, "but do not know how to farm profitably."

ently going down, houses get out of repair and rot down; fences are burned, as it is easier to move them than to split wood; ditches are allowed to fill up; grass and shrub bushes constantly encroach on the open land, and, in fact, in all parts of Georgia where the rent system is allowed, it is a saying that the negro renter's foot is poison to the land."[15]

Correspondents said that renters know nothing about rotation of crops or other methods of conservation,[16] that renters are an unstable class, who remain only a year or two in one place and exhaust the soil without putting anything back into it.[17] Many stated that they permitted renting only because it was impossible to employ day laborers or croppers.[18]

One of the inquiries in the Plantation Schedules sought to elicit information as to the relative effect of the two forms of tenure on production, conservation of the soil, and the progress of the tenants. Planters' replies usually took the form of concrete illustrations. A Screven County planter,[19] operating 16,000 acres with one hundred and forty-two share tenants, in 1910 performed the following experiment with a view of demonstrating to the tenants the superiority of the share arrangement. A sixty acre tract of land of uniform grade was selected and divided into two farms. This land was turned over to one of the "two-horse" tenants under an arrangement by which the two tracts were worked with the same animals and tools, and a like amount of fertilizers. The only point of difference was that on one of the farms the tenant worked according to his own ideas, on the other he followed the directions of the manager. The supervised farm produced twenty-two bales of cotton, the other twelve. Nevertheless, the negro left the plantation at the end of the year because the manager refused to allow him to stay as a renter. No

---

[15] *Inquiries III*, 1906, Letter from Muscogee County.

[16] *Ibid*, Letter from Baldwin County: Planter prefers the share system, "because the land is not relinquished to tenant, and I can rotate more intelligently. By nature, a negro who rents outright is fond of exercising full and unrestricted power to do as he sees fit, and but few, very few, have any idea at all of rotation or any other means of preserving the soil. In short, land left to his judgment will go to the bowwows, or the Atlantic Ocean, in this hill country." All of this planter's tenants have been with him twenty years or more.

[17] *Ibid*, Letter from Richmond County.

[18] *Ibid*, Letters from Bibb, Hancock and Baldwin Counties.

[19] *Plantation Schedules*, 1911, No. 10.

stronger evidence could be produced that share farming is better for landlord and tenant, and that profit is a secondary consideration with the tenant. On the share farm, the tenant's gross share was eleven bales, from which he had to pay only his own support and half the fertilizer bill. On the second farm, his net return after paying rent was not more than nine bales, and from this he was obliged to pay the entire fertilizer bill, and support for his work animal, besides wear and tear and interest on the investment in stock and tools.

A Dougherty County planter [20] rented to one Stewart for about ten consecutive years, during all of which time the renter was never out of debt. Losing patience, the planter refused to "carry" him longer, and induced him to work on shares, with the same land and mule. The darky was soon free of debt and saved enough to buy a new mule and a buggy. He then felt ready to set up again as a renter, and, the planter refusing to rent, he left the place. After two years he returned to his original employer, bankrupt, began again as a share tenant, and in the summer of 1911 was free of debt.

Scores of such cases are recorded in "Plantation Schedules." In nearly every case the share tenant admits making more profits under the share system, but utterly denies that the owner's direction is responsible for the result.[21] The superior profits are attributed to the fact that croppers are put on better grades of land and that more fertilizers are used. Several tenants were found during the summer who admitted the advantage of wise direction. On one plantation visited, a mulatto was acting as foreman.[22] This man without hesitation stated that the mass of negroes were not qualified for independent renting, and that they desired to rent principally for the reason that in that status they had the unrestricted control over a mule to ride on Sundays.

Viewed in the proper light, only one form of tenancy exists in Georgia, namely, renting. The share tenant is in reality a day laborer. Instead of receiving weekly or monthly wages, he is

---

[20] *Ibid,* No. 25.
[21] *Ibid,* No. 7. Five such conversations are here reported. All explicitly admitted greater profits from the share system, but as emphatically denied that this resulted from supervision. Similarly No. 39.
[22] *Ibid,* No. 16.

paid a share of the crop raised on the tract of land for which he is responsible. Absolute control of the crop remains in the hands of the landlord. He deducts all charges for support of the tenant, and turns over the balance to him. It is true that the typical wage method of working in gangs gave way on the whole to individual holdings, but this change did not eliminate supervision. Instead of standing over the gang of laborers constantly, the owner or his representative now rides from farm to farm, watching the state of the crop, deciding on the method of cultivation, requiring the tenant to keep up the property, and above all enforcing regularity of work. Supervision was to some extent weakened by the change, but it is questionable whether in a free-negro regime the slackening of discipline materially affects production. The wage hand was an uncertain factor in that he was liable to disappear on any pay day; the cropper is obliged to stay at least during an entire year, or forfeit his profits. This steadiness imparted to the tenant by self-interest doubtless compensates for the slight relaxing of discipline. Indeed, the share system is not altogether incompatible with gang labor. Many planters hold that in large-scale production of cotton the really crucial point of difference between the share and renting systems is in connection with the preparation of the soil. When the plantation is organized on a share basis, the planter furnishes heavy plows and harrows and strong teams, and all the share farms are prepared just as if they were one farm, laborers and teams going in gangs straight over the plantation, regardless of the individual holdings. In this way every portion of the plantation receives similar treatment. Division into individual holdings is made after preparation and planting. Furthermore, as the croppers are under full control as to their time, they are sometimes worked in gangs during the cultivating season. For instance, if the manager sees that the crop of one of his share tenants is being neglected, he may send a gang of other croppers to put things to rights, charging the extra time against the negligent cropper's half of the crop. This sort of cooperation is not practicable with renters. In the first place, the planter does not have control of their time. In the second place, renters' work-animals and tools are of varying degrees of efficiency, many tenants owning only the most wretched stock and implements. It would not be fair to combine poor animals with good ones and give the inefficient renter the benefit of the services of the equipment of the efficient men. A third difficulty is that renters are independent and differ in their ideas about farming, for example, about the amount of fertilizers that may profitably be used.

When it is once realized that the share system finds place only on plantations under close supervision, that the share tenant is really a day laborer, and that his holding is not a farm but a section of a well-ordered unit, it should be manifest that there is little cause for alarm on account of the decline in the percentage of farms operated by owners, and the growth of tenancy in Georgia. While in 1910, 65.4 per cent. of all farms were tenant holdings, more than half of these (56 per cent.) were share farms. Furthermore, during the past decade, the share tenants increased at a more rapid rate than the cash tenants,[23] and there is reason to believe that the negro element of cash tenants is destined to become a progressively smaller factor in the situation than at present.

The law of Georgia sustains the position that the share tenant is only a day laborer and not a real tenant. Of course, the law simply crystallizes the actual economic facts as they have worked out. In 1872, the Supreme Court in the case of Appling vs. Odum[24] held:

"There is an obvious distinction between a cropper and a tenant. One has a possession of the premises, exclusive of the landlord, the other has not. The one has a right for a fixed time, the other has only a right to go on the land to plant, work and gather the crop. The possession of the land is with the owner as against the cropper. The case made in the record is not the case of a tenant. The owner of the land furnished the land and the supplies. The share of the cropper was to remain on the land and to be subject to the advances of the owner for supplies. *The case of the cropper is rather a mode of paying wages than a tenancy.* The title to the crop subject to the wages is in the owner of the land."

The important words have been italicised, in which the court expressed the opinion that a share hand is a wage earner, not a

[23] See Table, *ante,* p. 57.
[24] 46 *Georgia Reports,* pp. 584–585.

tenant, or renter.   This decision has been the basis of all subsequent rulings as to the relations of landlords and tenants in Georgia.   The view was reiterated in 1878[25] when the court held that ''Where one is employed to work for part of the crop, the relation of landlord and tenant does not arise.''   Ten years later the court defined with great clearness the position of the share hand :[26]

"Where an owner of land furnishes it with supplies and other like necessaries, keeping general supervision over the farm, and agrees to pay a certain portion of the crop to the laborer for his work, the laborer is a cropper, and judgments or liens cannot sell his part of the crop until the landlord is fully paid, but where there is a renting, and the relation of landlord and tenant exists, an older judgment will subject the renter's crop . . . [both parties] swore that Plunkett [the tenant] rented the land from Almand for a specified rent. The land, therefore, was in possession of Plunkett, the tenant, and not in Almand, the owner. The work was not done under Almand's superintendence and direction. Almand had no control over the land, and the crop made on the land was not to go in payment to Plunkett for his labor in making the crop. He was therefore not a cropper as defined in 46 Ga. 583 (Appling vs. Odum.)"

It should now be clear that in economic significance, and in their practical and legal aspects, renting and share tenancy are as wide apart as the poles.   The cropper is a day laborer, works under constant direction, has no exclusive right to the premises or title to the crop he produces.   The renter, on the other hand, is a real tenant.   The court has explicitly held[27] that the landlord has no right to enter on the tenant's farm against his will to interfere with the crops.   The tenant has exclusive possession of the premises for the time being and entire control over his crops. It is scarcely necessary to point out that the reason underlying this distinction is that, in the case of the cropper, the landlord is the sole capitalist and entrepreneur.   Everything necessary to make the crop is supplied by him; while, in the case of the tenant, a fixed rental per acre is paid the landlord, and the landlord's connection with the tenant's farm ceases there.

---

[25] 61 *Georgia Reports*, p. 488.
[26] 80 *Georgia Reports*, p. 95.
[27] 75 *Georgia Reports*, p. 274.

CHAPTER V

THE MOUNTAIN COUNTIES AND THE UPPER PIED-
MONT: ECONOMIC HISTORY AND LAND
TENURE MOVEMENTS

In the preceding discussion of the changes that have come in the agricultural labor arrangements since the sixties, Georgia has been treated as a unit, but the readjustment has not been uniform in all sections of the state. Georgia embraces several physiographic divisions which differ widely in climate, soil properties, and health conditions. The physiography of these areas has determined their historical development and the character of the present population, some of the sections having been settled by cotton planters and their slaves, others having been developed by small white farmers. The labor system of those areas where whites predominate presents a sharp contrast to the system prevalent in the sections containing black majorities. The state falls into five natural divisions, the Mountainous region, consisting of the two most northern tiers of counties, the Upper Piedmont, between the mountain division and the Black Belt, the Black Belt, extending across Middle and Southwest Georgia, the Wiregrass region of South Central and Southeast Georgia, and the Coast counties.[1]

The Mountain counties are cut off from the Upper Piedmont because they are insignificant in agriculture and will be given only passing notice. The Coast counties are separated from the Wiregrass region because in the character of the population and status of the agricultural classes the two sections are totally dissimilar. The Coast counties are of prime importance historically and

---

[1] See Map, app., p. 127. These divisions will be designated as Group I, Group II, etc.

would be a fit subject for monographic study.   They were not included in the investigative work of 1911, and the present writer
knows little at first hand of conditions there.

The essential differences in population and land tenure among
the five sections are given in the following tables:

*Table Showing Population of the Five Sections in 1870 and 1910, Percent-
age of Increase, Per Capita Wealth of Total Population and of Negroes [2]
in 1910*

	1870			1910					
	Total population.	Per cent. white	Per cent. black	Total population	Per cent. white	Per cent. black	Per cent. increase 1870—1910	Per capita wealth	Per capita wealth of negroes
Group I...............	99,305	89.1	10.9	157,819	92.6	7.4	58.9	$184.76	$30.30
Group II.............	273,356	68.6	31.4	692,779	71.0	29.0	153.4	285.94	25.44
Group III.............	656,424	40.0	60.0	1,166,924	38.9	61.1	77.4	226.58	23.75
Group IV.............	84,333	70.0	30.0	460,341	61.6	38.4	445.8	224.16	31.27
Group V	68,701	37.0	63.0	129,168	41.4	58.6	88.0	364.00	27.78

Table Showing Land Tenure, 1910, in the Five Groups [3]

	Total farms.	Farms operated by owners	Cash tenants	Share tenants
Group I...	22,869	12,368 (54.08)	1,003 (4.39)	9,498 (41.53)
Group II.............	73,540	25,080 (34.11)	12,613 (17.15)	35,847 (48.74)
Group III............. ...	137,512	35,045 (25.48)	57,147 (41.56)	45,320 (32.96)
Group IV.................	53,138	24,387 (45.90)	11,134 (20.92)	17,617 (33.15)
Group V.................	4,152	3,428 (82.56)	436 (10.50)	288 (6.94)

The tables reveal strikingly dissimilar conditions in the several groups.   The proportion of whites in the population varies
from 92.6 per cent. in Group I to 38.9 per cent. in Group III (the
Black Belt) ; the percentage of increase of population since the
Civil War varies from 58.9 per cent. in one section to 445.8 per

---

[2] This table was compiled from U. S. Census, 1870, the Bulletin of the 1910
Census on Georgia Population, and the 1910 *Report* of the Comptroller General
of Georgia, Tables 15 and 17.   Of course, the data does not appear in the Census reports in the above shape.   It was necessary to rearrange the counties into
the proper groups and work out the additions and percentages.

[3] U. S. Census, 1910, *Bulletin on Agriculture in Georgia.*   Minor changes may
be-made in the Census data before final publication.

cent. in another, the percentage of farms operated by owners to all farms runs from 82.56 per cent. in Group V to 25.48 per cent. in the third division. Share tenants are in the ascendency in Groups I and II, while cash tenants form the most important element numerically in the agricultural population of Group III. The per capita wealth is much higher in some sections than in others. It seems, therefore, worth while to inquire into the causes of these divergencies.

Of the five divisions, the Coast is at once the oldest and the most backward in agriculture. In 1910 the proportion of negroes to the total population was high and the percentage of farms operated by owners higher than in any other group.

The Black Belt, Group III, is the oldest cotton region of the state, the most important historically, and the largest in area. The belt is so laid off as to include all of the ante-bellum plantation counties (except those of the Coast), and also all other counties which have acquired a black majority since 1870. Several counties with white majorities are unavoidably included in this group. It will be noted that the percentage of blacks in the total population has increased since 1870. This is the region where most of the large plantations are found.

The Upper Piedmont, Group II, was being settled contemporaneously with the Black Belt, but by a wholly different element, the small farmer. All these counties had a white majority in 1870, and the proportion of whites to blacks has increased during the last forty years. While this section contains only about fifteen per cent. of the total area of Georgia, it is a region of great wealth, being surpassed in this respect only by the Black Belt, which, though three times as large in area, can boast of but 25 per cent. more wealth. The per capita wealth of the Upper Piedmont is far higher than in the other sections.[4] The population of this region has grown with great rapidity, having increased 153.4 per cent. since 1870. This growth is partly due to the fact

---

[4] The high *per capita* of the Coast Counties is due to the fact that the district is small, containing only six counties, and of these, one, Chatham, furnishes sixty per cent. of the population and about eighty per cent. of the wealth, Savannah real estate being the principal item. If Chatham be omitted, the *per capita* for the other counties is $220.08.

that this part of Georgia has been the center of the recent industrial development.

In point of economic development, the Wiregrass, Group IV, is the newest part of Georgia. Until the use of commercial fertilizers revolutionized the cotton industry, the Wiregrass was not highly esteemed as farming land. For many years lumbering was the leading industry. This section is now developing more rapidly than any other part of the state, its easily cultivated land, offered at reasonable prices, attracting thousands of farmers not only from the Mountain counties and the Black Belt, but from other states. The majority of the population is white.

A. Group I: The Mountain Counties

The southern extremities of the Appalachian chain run across the northernmost tiers of Georgia counties, the Blue Ridge in the northeastern corner and a number of ranges in the northwestern corner. The Blue Ridge section includes ten of the counties of this Group. The valleys of the Blue Ridge vary from 1,600 to 1,800 feet above sea level, several of the peaks running over 4,000 feet in height. In the northwestern part of the Group, the valleys range from 600 feet upwards, while the highest peaks are about 2,500 feet above sea level.[5] The lower counties of the northwestern section, Floyd, Polk, and Bartow, are important in agriculture and are included in the second group.

The soil of the northwestern counties is largely limestone, well suited to cereal production. The Blue Ridge counties are metamorphic, and here the fruit and vegetable industries have grown to important proportions. The mineral wealth of the Mountain counties is great and is now being developed. Coal, iron ore, and marble are present in abundance.

Little cotton is produced in this group, less than two per cent. of the total crop of the state being raised here. The soil and climate are unfavorable to staple production. The region is characterized by the small white farming element and a self-suf-

---

[5] *Georgia Historical and Industrial*, 1901, pp. 36–40, 148. Published by Georgia Department of Agriculture. U. S. Census, 1880, VI, *Cotton Production*, pp. 276–442. Both publications contain physiographic maps of Georgia and detailed descriptions of every county.

ficing economy. So large a proportion of the soil is mountainous and hence unfit for agriculture that the population is relatively sparse and land values low. In only ten counties is the average value of farm lands above ten dollars, and in some counties it is much lower.[6]

The counties of this group, except Rabun and Habersham, were in Cherokee country, acquired from the Indians so recently as 1837. This tract, the last of the Indian lands, was surveyed into lots in 1832 and distributed by a lottery system the same year.[7] Political and legal complications prevented the expulsion of the Cherokees until 1837, but in spite of their presence, and in defiance of law, settlers poured in, attracted by the discovery of gold in the mountains. The soil was unattractive for agricultural purposes, but the gold fever drew thousands of adventurers, many of whom remained after the short-lived boom was over and lands had fallen in price. The forty-acre lots were sold by the original drawers for from ten to twenty dollars, as soon as it was known that the gold was very limited in quantity. The immigrants to this last Georgia frontier were of Scotch-Irish extraction, coming in from Virginia and North Carolina. Many Middle Georgia people were also among the early comers. They were a crude, uneducated people, and in the north-eastern counties have remained to the present day almost untouched by the civilizing influences of the lower country. The opening of the state railroad from Atlanta to Chattanooga, in 1851, effected a great transformation in the northwest. The northeast, or Blue Ridge section, remained without railway facilities until the seventies, when the Southern Railway and its branches opened up the country. During the last few decades, Group I has been declining in population. Eight counties, seven of which were in the Blue Ridge region, had a smaller population in 1910 than in 1900,[8] the loss ranging from 9 to 26 per cent. Three counties show a healthy growth. Many mountaineers have migrated to the Wiregrass section, but the principal cause of the loss of popu-

---

[6] U. S. Census, 1910, *Bulletin: Agriculture in Georgia*, map, p. 2.   The map is reproduced in the appendix, *post*, p. 129.

[7] Smith, G. G., *Story of Georgia and the Georgia People* (Atlanta, 1900), pp. 422–423.

[8] U. S. Census, 1910, *Bulletin: Georgia Population*, map, p. 6.

lation is to be found in the fact that the mountain people are the source of labor supply for the cotton mills.[9]

The important facts as to the tendencies in the farming situation are shown in the following table:

LAND TENURE IN GROUP I [10]
ALL FARMERS

Year	Total farms	Per cent. of all farms in state	Operated by owners	Cash tenants	Share tenants
1880	15,862	11.43	66.74	2.17	31.09
1890	17,632	10.32	61.78	1.91	36.31
1900	21,915	9.76	56.60	3.13	40.27
1910	22,869	7.85	54.08	4.39	41.53

WHITE FARMERS

Year	Total farms	Per cent. of all farms in state	Operated by owners	Cash tenants	Share tenants
1900	20,802	14.60	58.33	3.02	38.65
1910	21,631	12.83	55.40	4.30	40.30

NEGRO FARMERS

Year	Total farms	Per cent. of all farms in state	Operated by owners	Cash tenants	Share tenants
1900	1,113	1.34	24.80	5.20	70.00
1910	1,238	1.01	30.77	5.81	63.42

The negro farmer is an insignificant element in this group, 95 per cent. of all farms being operated by whites. The percentage of farms worked by owners is high, but is decreasing, due to the fact that many small farmers have sold their unprofitable holdings and migrated to other sections of the state, their small farms tending to be merged into large units. There is practically no cash renting. This prevalence of share tenancy is characteristic of those groups of counties containing white majorities, as will appear in the more detailed discussion of tenure in Group II.

B. Group II: The Upper Piedmont

This group contains all those counties of the Piedmont Plateau south of the mountains whose population in 1910 was predom-

---

[9] *Reports on Georgia Plantation Districts,* I, p. 3.
[10] This Table was compiled from Census reports. See *post* p. 122.

inantly white. The map[11] shows this region as a belt extending across the state, two counties deep on the Savannah River and widening to a depth of five counties on the Alabama line. The counties of the group are similar in their physical characteristics, except that Floyd, Bartow, and Polk are geologically of the northwestern group. The Piedmont or metamorphic region extends southward to the fall line of the rivers. This line passes through Richmond, Bibb, and Muscogee counties. The surface of the country is rolling and hilly, though rarely so broken as to make agriculture unprofitable. The red hill is characteristic of the section. Red sandy, red clayey, and gray sandy soils are found in every county.[12]

The settlement of the Upper Piedmont began in 1784[13] with the laying off of Franklin county on the Savannah river. All lands east of the Oconee river were distributed under a "Head-Rights" system. Each settler was offered two hundred acres of land as his individual head-right, and fifty acres in addition for each child or slave he brought. Later a limit of one thousand acres per family was set. As the land was good, the region was settled rapidly, the first county, Franklin, having a population of 9,156 whites and 1,041 negroes in 1810, though the county had been greatly reduced in area by parts being laid off into new counties. The settlers were Scotch-Irish people from the Carolinas. Their fathers had taken part in the great movement of the Scotch-Irish from Pennsylvania down the Shenandoah Valley.[14] They were typical frontiersmen, rough, uncultured, without property, but of a sturdy, independent spirit. They settled down as small farmers, producing practically everything they consumed. With each new cession of Indian lands, these small farmers or their sons pushed westward, until in 1826 the Alabama line was reached. At every stage of their westward march, their numbers were reinforced by the non-slaveholding farmers who were being gradually dispossessed in the Black Belt. This region, being cut up into relatively small farms, worked by white owners, escaped in large measure the exploitative system of agri-

---

[11] See *post*, p. 127.
[12] *Georgia Historical and Industrial*, p. 153.
[13] Watkins, Robert and George, *Digest of the Laws of the State of Georgia* (Philadelphia, 1800), p. 291.
[14] Smith, *Story of Georgia*, pp. 152–153.

culture which dominated the Black Belt.[15]   The small farmers
had not the means to effect the transformation from farmer to
planter, after the invention of the cotton gin made large-scale
cotton production possible.   The planters tended to move in a
southwesterly direction, beginning at the Savannah river, think-
ing the land further north to be infertile, so that few negroes
were brought into the Upper Piedmont.   The section was distinctly a white one, only 31.4 per cent. of the total population in
1870 being colored.   This proportion has declined: in 1910 the
blacks were 29 per cent. of the whole.[16]

It has been customary to regard southern ante-bellum society
as consisting of only two classes besides slaves, the planter aris-
tocracy and the "poor whites."   Here in the Piedmont region
of Georgia was a third element, the small farmer, quite as distinct
from the mountaineer and "piney-woods cracker" as he was
from the planter.   He belonged to a middle class, in every way
comparable to his contemporaries in the free North and West.[17]

The following table indicates the direction of the tenure movement at the four Census periods:

LAND TENURE IN GROUP II
ALL FARMERS

Year	Total farms	Per cent. of all farmers in state	Operated by owners	Cash tenants	Share tenants
1880	38,292	27.63	57.70	5.63	36.67
1890	44,073	25.76	47.34	7.52	45.14
1900	57,841	25.74	37.95	13.73	48.32
1910	73,540	25.24	34.11	17.15	48.74

WHITE FARMERS

1900	45,060	31.79	45.70	12.13	42.17
1910	55,245	32.76	41.67	14.49	43.84

COLORED FARMERS

1900	12,781	15.43	10.73	19.36	69.91
1910	18,295	14.93	11.22	25.18	63.60

[15] Brooks, R. P., *Race Relations in the Eastern Piedmont Region of Georgia*, in *Political Science Quarterly*, June, 1911, p. 200.

[16] See Table, *ante*, p. 70.

[17] Stone, A. H., in *The South in the Building of the Nation*, V, p. 139.   The author scouts as absurd the idea that non-slaveholders were an economic cypher in the South.   In the upper Piedmont region, 200 by 400 miles in extent, there were a million of these people and only a hundred thousand negroes.

The number of farms increased nearly 100 per cent. in the three decades after 1880. Farms operated by owners, while absolutely increasing at a fair rate, declined relatively from 57.70 to 34.11 per cent. of all farms. Several explanations may be offered of this fact. Small farms, owned by their operators, having been the rule throughout the history of the section, and the land having been practically all taken up prior to 1870, there was not so large an opportunity for the spread of small ownership as was the case in the Black Belt or the Wiregrass. Secondly, since the border counties on the southern edge of the group partake to some extent of the characteristics of the Black Belt, a considerable number of large farms or plantations existed there in antebellum days. These plantations underwent the process of nominal disintegration described in a former chapter, wage earners becoming "croppers," and, being classed as tenants, the percentage of farms operated by owners was lowered. A concrete instance of this sort may be cited. The writer visited a plantation of 1,500 acres in Coweta county.[18] The owner lived in the town of Newnan, his plantation being managed by a resident overseer. The overseer closely supervised the laboring population, consisting of twenty-five croppers and five day laborers. The Census enumerates this plantation as twenty-six farms; one, that of the owner with his five laborers, the remaining twenty-five being those of the share tenants. That the plantation was essentially a unit is clear from the nature of the supervision. The kind and acreage of all crops to be grown was determined by the landlord, who also fixed the days when the tenants must work, as in the case of his day laborers; work was begun and ended by the tap of the plantation bell, and all of the crops were marketed by the landlord.[19]

A third reason why ownership has not been widely extended in this region is that, because of the high type of farming and the good treatment the soil has received at the hands of small white farmers, lands have so appreciated in value that tenant farmers are unable to buy. Nine of the eleven counties in Georgia which in 1910 showed an average land value of from $25 to $50 per acre

---

[18] *Plantation Schedules,* 1911, no. 37.
[19] *Ibid,* no. 38 is a similar case.

(the highest values in the state) were in this group.[20]   The extent to which the section is developed is indicated by the fact that it is the region of the densest population in the state, and that in nine counties 90 to 100 per cent. of the land area is in farms, and in thirteen other counties from 80 to 90 per cent.   Between 1900 and 1910 real estate values in Franklin, Jackson, Madison, Walton, and Hart counties (considered as a group) advanced 253 per cent.[21]   Cases are reported of tenants' having cash to buy land, but being prevented from so doing by the high prices. Share farmers, however, are able to stock rented farms, so that a comparatively high type of renter is to be found in the district. The writer was impressed by the fact that the feeling in this group as to the evils of renting is not so pronouncedly hostile as in other sections.[22]   One large planter stated that his renters made as much profits as the wage earners or croppers, "because they are a superior class of whites."[23]   All of the plantation schedules taken in this group contain statements that the planter prefers white to negro labor,[24] but the consensus was that the negroes are of a higher type in this district than in the Black Belt, an opinion which is accounted for by the fact that they are numerically a small element in the population, and have felt the effect of white stimulus and competition.[25]   Many negroes are felt to deserve the position of renters.   Still another reason why renting is not felt to be so unsatisfactory is that the rent contracts are not the usual one-year arrangements, but commonly run for a term of years.   Planters say that this makes for good farming.   The contracts are in writing and contain provisions intended to prevent the exhaustion and deterioration of the soil.[26]

---

[20] See Map, *post*, p. 129.

[21] *Reports on Georgia Plantation Districts*, 1911, Report no. 2, p. 2.

[22] *Ibid*, pp. 2–3.

[23] *Plantation Schedules*, 1911, no. 38.

[24] *Ibid*, nos. 1, 3, 37, 38.

[25] *Reports on Georgia Plantation Districts, Report* no. 2, p. 5.   Brooks, *op. cit.*, pp. 204–7.

[26] *Plantation Schedules*, 1911, no. 3.   The following is an extract from the contract used.   After reciting that the contract shall run from Nov. 1, 1908 to Nov. 1, 1912, the tenant "also agrees and promises to look carefully after the orchard on said farm and to plow it up at least twice during each year, also to keep the weeds and grass cut off the terraces and the low places on the terraces

The most significant fact revealed by the statistical table is the relative positions of the two forms of tenancy. Comparatively few tenant farms are operated by renters, or cash tenants, the percentage of share tenants having been higher in 1880 than in any of the groups, and having maintained its lead up to the present. Especially is this true in the case of negro tenants, 63.60 per cent. of their farms being held on this tenure in 1910. The explanation of the prevalence of "cropping" is that the majority of Upper Piedmont farmers who employ labor live on their farms, are in a position to give effective supervision, and insist on the share arrangement. Of the white farms, 14.49 per cent. and of the black 25.18 per cent. are in the hands of independent renters. As has been said, some of these renters are of a superior type, but it is stated that absenteeism is tending to increase in some of the counties,[27] and as absenteeism and independent renting go together, it is likely that a part of the renters of the group are of the same sort as those of the Black Belt.

Some confusion in the statistics of this group arises from the fact that the Census classifies as share tenants the "third-and-fourth" share farmers, i. e., those who pay a third of the corn and a fourth of the cotton as rent. This system, once common throughout Georgia, has disappeared except in Groups I and II. Planters regard this form of tenancy as renting, because the third-and-fourth farmer supplies his own stock, tools, and support, and is not subject to supervision. A majority of white share tenants are said to be of this class, while the negro tenants are said to be "croppers," or half-share farmers.[28]

In 1860, the Black Belt produced 82.87 per cent. of all the cotton grown in Georgia. Every succeeding decade has witnessed a decrease in the relative importance of this belt: in 1910 it produced 57.98 per cent. of the entire crop. The Upper Piedmont,

---

filled up, also to keep the banks of the creeks and branches cleaned off down to the water, . . . also to furnish all necessary labor free of charge to terrace the land, provided the said party of the first part furnishes the terracer and terracing implements; and also to make all necessary repairs [on the buildings] . . . all the above to be done as part of the rent. The said [tenant] also agrees to sow as much as [blank] acres each year in wheat or oats as the said party of the first part may direct, etc."

[27] *Reports on Georgia Plantation Districts*, Report no. 1, p. 4.
[28] *Ibid*, Report no. 2, p. 4.

on the contrary, produced only 88,670 bales in 1860, or 12.67 per cent. of the total crop. In the fifty years following, while the Black Belt has barely doubled her output, the Piedmont section has increased hers 377 per cent.[29]   This development is one of the most noteworthy facts in the post-bellum history of the state, and is attributable to a variety of causes. First in importance is the character of the population, a small white farmer element. The superiority of the white farming was indicated by the Census of 1880,[30] wherein it appeared that the per acre product of Group II was .398 bales, while in the Black Belt, Group III, the average was .286 bales. This superiority has been maintained. Secondly, the majority of the farmers in ante-bellum days did their own work, having few slaves; hence their operations were less disturbed by the *débacle* of emancipation, and recovery was quick. In the third place, commercial fertilizers made cotton production much more profitable in this section,[31] as the best cotton lands were further south. The comparative absence of independent negro farmers, the rapid extension of railroads, and the use of superior farming implements,[32] favored the development of the group.

A study has been made of the relative conditions of the black population in certain counties of this group in comparison with conditions prevailing in contiguous counties of the Black Belt.[33] It was shown that the influence of a preponderant white population was altogether favorable to the colored farmers. The per capita wealth of negroes in the white counties was higher than in the black counties, the percentage of landowning negroes was in inverse ratio to their numbers—highest where they were the smallest element of the population; the croppers or share tenants made greater profits than did the renters, and the school facili-

---

[29] See Table *post*, p. 124 for a compilation showing the acreage and production of cotton in Georgia.   The five Groups are given separately for each Census year since 1860.   The table shows the percentage each Group's production has been of the whole output, the relative acreages and the product per acre since 1880. This table was compiled from Census reports.

[30] *Ibid.*

[31] Avery, I. W., *History of Georgia, 1850–1881* (New York, 1881), p. 643.   Grady, Henry W., in *Harper's Magazine*, October, 1881.

[32] U. S. Department of Agriculture, *Report*, 1876, p. 127. "Wherever white labor is predominant, labor-saving implements are coming into general use."

[33] Brooks, *op. cit.*

ties of the negroes were better in the white counties.   That these
conclusions are applicable to the entire sections may be seen from
the fact that 11.22 per cent. of the negro farms of Group II are
operated by owners, while for the Black Belt the percentage is
9.13.   The negroes' *per capita* wealth is higher in the Upper
Piedmont than in the Black Belt.

CHAPTER VI

THE BLACK BELT: ECONOMIC HISTORY AND LAND TENURE MOVEMENTS

The Black Belt of Georgia embraces a variety of physiographic divisions and soils.[1] That part of the Belt which lies north of the fall line of the rivers is a rolling and hilly country of metamorphic soil, as it is a continuance of the Upper Piedmont. Below the fall line a narrow strip of sandhills crosses the state, and then comes a belt of oak, hickory, and long leaf pine uplands, covering about a third of the Black Belt.   The remainder of the section is a limesink and wiregrass region. Below the fall line the country is generally level and the soil gray and sandy, though red hills and a considerable amount of clay lands occur.[2]

The settlement of the Black Belt counties extended over a century, beginning about the middle of the eighteenth century, on the Savannah River, and pushing westward by regular stages. Successive waves of frontiersmen, small farmers, and cotton planters moved in a westward and southwestward direction until shortly before the Civil War the extreme southwestern counties were filled. Burke, Columbia, and Wilkes Counties were the scene of the first frontier settlements in Georgia, after the peopling of the coast.   Immigrants direct from Europe occupied the coast region, but these middle Georgia counties were settled by Americans pushing down from Virginia and the Carolinas. Burke County is believed to have had white inhabitants before Oglethorpe came in 1733, probably Indian traders from the Carolinas.

Three years before the Revolution there was obtained from the

---

[1] U. S. Census, 1880, VI, *Cotton Production*, p. 277, Map.
[2] *Georgia Historical and Industrial*, pp. 156–162.

Creeks[3] a cession of land from which many counties were carved, such as Wilkes, Elbert, and Lincoln. This land was at once thrown open for settlement under the headrights system. The early comers were from the same class of people that filled the Upper Piedmont. The first wave of frontiersmen was followed at the close of the Revolution by men in better circumstances, Virginians constituting the most important element.[4] Exhaustion of their tobacco fields was the immediate cause of the migration. As in the case of the settlers of the Upper Piedmont, the new comers practiced for a generation a self-sufficing economy: cattle raising, diversified agriculture, and home manufactures characterized their industrial life. But the invention of the cotton gin in 1793, and the development of the cotton industry in the two decades following, revolutionized the economic life of the Lincoln and Wilkes County farmers. Being men of large ideas, possessing more property than their fellows in the Upper Piedmont, and occupying a soil admirably suited to cotton culture, the Virginian element quickly evolved into large-scale producers of cotton. Gradually the holdings of the less efficient were acquired, cattle ranges were put to the plow, and the small farmer and herdsman moved westward to squat on fresh lands. Exhausting their original holdings, the planters soon pushed on after the frontiersmen and small farmers, bought their clearings and created new plantations. This process involved social differentiation, society becoming highly stratified, with the planter element of course at the top. Their economic dominance was reflected in political life and presently the planters controlled the State and wielded a powerful influence in national politics during the ascendency of the cotton South just prior to the sixties.[5]

Something of the process above sketched is indicated in the population statistics of the eastern counties of the Belt.

---

[3] Phillips, U. B., *Georgia and State Rights* (Washington, 1902), p. 39.

[4] Gilmer, G. R., *Georgians*, Introduction, pp. 5–6. These Virginians were not the ordinary pioneer type of settlers, but appear to have been people of some consequence. They transplanted to Georgia the contemporary Virginian civilization and were to some extent a distinct element in the population.

[5] Smith, *Story of Georgia*, pp. 126–145, 196–200.

Typical Counties in the Black Belt, showing the Decline of the White Element and Increase of Negroes.

Year	Lincoln		Warren		Hancock		Greene		Putnam	
	White	Black	White	Black	White	Black	White	Black	White	Black
1800	3326	1440	6752	2077	9605	4851	7007	3664	....	......
1810	2331	2224	5659	3066	6343	6431	6398	5281	6771	3258
1820	3378	3080	6530	4100	5847	6887	6599	6990	8208	7267
1830	2824	3321	6152	4794	4603	7217	5026	7523	5513	7748
1840	2527	3368	5176	4313	3697	5932	4641	7049	3741	6519
1850	2187	3811	6158	6237	4210	7368	4744	8324	3300	7494
1860	1675	3791	4347	5473	3871	8173	4229	8423	2956	7169

A similar table for counties in the Upper Piedmont shows a very different tendency, whites outnumbering blacks from the beginning of settlement and their preponderance increasing at every census period up to the present time. In the Black Belt, in the first two decades of the nineteenth century the small farmer was the dominant element, outnumbering the planters and their slaves. By 1830, however, in many counties negroes outnumbered whites, and during the next decade forged far ahead. Each census period showed a steady absolute decline of whites and a large increase of negroes, indicating the departure of the small farmer and the increase in the size of slave- and land-holdings of the planters. The Indian frontier rapidly receded in the first quarter of the nineteenth century. The frontiersmen were usually on the border waiting for the first signal to move over.[6] The planter was not far behind. Gradually the entire region now known as the Black Belt was settled in this way. Early County in extreme southwest Georgia was laid off as early as 1818, and included all that section of the State. Population was, however, very thin, until the Central of Georgia Railway opened up the country in the fifties. By 1860 the plantation regime was established in that section.[7]

The subordination of all other agricultural interests to large-scale, slave-produced cotton entailed the abandonment of the di-

---

[6] Phillips, U. B., *Plantation and Frontier*, II, pp. 187–193. An excellent contemporary account of the repeated movings of a small farmer.
[7] Smith, *Story of Georgia*, pp. 323–5, 400–405.

versified farming of the early period. While many planters produced practically everything necessary to their maintenance and comfort, yet, on the whole, not enough meat and corn were raised for home consumption, and large quantities of food stuffs were annually imported from the Middle West. Absence of diversification and rotation of crops quickly exhausted the primary fertility of the soil. DeBow, writing in 1854,[8] thus described Middle Georgia:

"The native soil of Middle Georgia is a rich, argillaceous loam, resting on a firm, clay foundation. In some of the richer counties, nearly all the lands have been cut down, and appropriated to tillage, a large maximum of which have been worn out, leaving a desolate picture for the traveller to behold. Decaying tenements, red, old hills, stripped of their native growth and virgin soil, and washed into deep gulleys, with here and there patches of Bermuda grass and stunted pine shrubs, struggling for subsistence on what was once one of the richest soils of America."

When the small number of the planters is considered, their dominance in the social, political, and economic life of the State is very striking. Of the 118,000 families in Georgia in 1860,[9] only 41,084 owned slaves. But 27,191 slaveowners possessed less than ten slaves each. Many of these slaveholders were of the professional and merchant classes of the town. Only 6,363 slaveowners had twenty or more slaves. These may be called the large-scale planters. Outside the circle of slaveowners, there were about 77,000 non-slaveholding families, most of whom were engaged in agriculture. Sharp variations existed in the condition of this element of the population. The stationary mountaineers never came into contact with slavery, the more active small farmers of the Black Belt moved into the Upper Piedmont, swelling the numbers of the dominant non-slaveholding element there, and assisting in building up a healthy region of small holdings. Still another element, unable to maintain themselves against the trend of the times, lacking the means and initiative to develop their small holdings or to get out of the region controlled by the planter, unwilling to work for wages in competition with slave labor, drifted

---

[8] DeBow, J. D. B., *Industrial Resources, Statistics, etc., of the United States,* N. Y., 1854. I, p. 363.
[9] U. S. Census, 1860, *Agriculture,* pp. 226–227.

into the barren and waste places, and there led a miserable existence. They were entirely cut off from the society of the planter
class and all it represented; they knew nothing of the movements
in the world about and beyond them; they accumulated nothing,
rarely acquired the rudiments of an education, and were utterly
disregarded by the other elements of society—even the slaves on
the large plantations holding them in contempt.

It is unnecessary to rehearse here the effects of Civil War and
emanicipation on the Black Belt. Former chapters have described the complete disorganization of labor, the attempt to revive the plantation regime, the rise of share farming and of renting. The older portion of the Black Belt responded very quickly
to the new influences. Negroes moved away by thousands, and
in order to prevent the depletion of the section of all laborers,
planters were obliged to rent lands, i. e., to abandon the plantation system. The rapidity of the subdivision of plantations in
the older part of the Black Belt is indicated by the following
table:

TABLE SHOWING THE DISINTEGRATION OF PLANTATIONS IN TYPICAL
COUNTIES OF THE OLDER SECTION OF THE BLACK BELT[19]

	10-20 acres		20-50 acres		50-100 acres		100-500 acres		500-1000 acres		1000 acres	
	1860–1870		1860–1870		1860–1870		1860–1870		1860–1870		1860–1870	
Burke	8	83	80	245	99	467	315	39	100	10	71	0
Oglethorpe	8	9	34	142	98	245	259	395	30	22	7	2
Putnam	1	2	6	39	16	100	157	161	65	9	29	0

The plantations of 1,000 acres or more almost entirely disappeared in ten years, as well as 80 per cent. of those in the 500 to
1,000 acre group, and in Burke County, the oldest of the group,
few in the next class survived.

The following table shows the principal facts in connection
with the matter of land tenure.

[19] *Ibid,* 1860, *Agriculture,* p. 196; 1870, *Wealth, Debt, and Taxation,* pp. 348–
349.

TABLE SHOWING LAND TENURE IN GROUP III[11]
ALL FARMERS

Year	Total farms	Per cent.of all farms in state	Operated by owners	Cash tenants	Share tenants
1880	66,778	48.18	45.48	21.00	33.52
1890	85,530	50.00	35.69	26.08	38.23
1900	108,246	48.16	30.10	40.54	29.36
1910	137,512	47.22	25.48	41.56	32.96

WHITE FARMERS

Year	Total farms	Per cent.of all farms in state	Operated by owners	Cash tenants	Share tenants
1900	49,470	34.90	54.80	29.40	15.80
1910	53,743	31.87	51.00	30.44	18.56

NEGRO FARMERS

Year	Total farms	Per cent.of all farms in state	Operated by owners	Cash tenants	Share tenants
1900	58,776	70.96	9.20	49.90	40.90
1910	83,769	68.35	9.13	48.69	42.18

While the number of farms increased more than one hundred per cent. in the Black Belt between 1880 and 1910, the number of farms operated by owners increased only 15.3 per cent. In the period which witnessed an absolute increase of only 4,675 additional farms operated by owners, tenant farms increased 66,109, or 181 per cent. Since more than 60 per cent. of all the Black Belt farms are operated by negroes, only 9.13 per cent. of whom operate their own farms, the low character of farming in this region may be inferred. This is the region of tenancy *par excellence,* 75 per cent. of all farms being in the hands of that class of farmers. Ninety per cent. of the negro farmers and nearly 50 per cent. of the white farmers are tenants.

The tendency has been for the whites of the Black Belt to leave the farm, the heads of families locating in the county towns, renting their lands to negroes or whites, and often going into merchandising, while the active sons have moved entirely out of the region to take business positions in cities. Many of the poorer whites have entered cotton mills. The Columbus (Muscogee County) district is a case in point. The counties in that part of the Belt have steadily lost their white population. Isolation of

---

[11] See *post.* p. 123.

white families, increasing criminality among the negroes, lack of school and church facilities, drove the whites into Columbus, a thriving city. There are more cotton mill operatives in Columbus than there are white farmers in nine surrounding counties on the Georgia side. It is well-known that nearly all of these operatives have come from adjacent rural districts.[12] Many other white families have moved to the Wiregrass country of Southeast Georgia. The better class of white owners are able to live on their rents; others, by combining the supply business with renting land to tenants, gain a competence. In this way the rural parts of the Black Belt have tended to grow blacker. Of all negro farms in the state, 68.35 per cent. were in 1910 in this region, whereas only 31.87 per cent. of all white farms are in the group. In 1870, negroes were 60 per cent. of the population, in 1910, 61.1 per cent.[13]

Reference to the land tenure table shows that the most numerous class of farmers are the cash tenants. This is the most fundamental point of difference between the agricultural labor situation here and in the white sections of the state, the share system being in the ascendency in the white regions. This fact has already been explained, but it will bear reiteration. Many landowners moved to the towns; a numerous class of merchant landowners came into existence; these absentee landlords everywhere rented their lands. Resident landlords, competing with absentees for laborers, were obliged in many cases to rent lands, or see them lie uncultivated. This movement reached its high-water mark in 1900, when 49.90 per cent. of negro farmers were cash tenants. These renters were practically independent of the planters. The slavery system had not made for conservation of the land, improved methods of agriculture, nor frugality. Slaves, of course, learned little of these matters. The necessary consequence was that when the freedmen became renters under no efficient supervision, in a part of the state where contact with small white farmers, with better habits and better methods of

---

[12] *Reports on Georgia Plantation Districts*, Report No. 9, pp. 2 and 3. The Black Belt is so great in extent that it was necessary in the investigation of 1911 to subdivide it into several districts. District Reports 3, 6, 7, 8, 9, 10, and part of 4 cover this Group.

[13] See Table, *ante*, p. 70.

farming, was impossible, they settled down to unintelligent cotton raising, living from hand to mouth, and became the poorest class of farmers to be found in any civilized country.

The table shows that in the decade 1890 to 1900 cash tenancy grew very rapidly, accompanied by a decline in share farming. It was predicted by those who favor the position of renter for the negro that share tenancy had reached its highest development and that the negroes were freeing themselves from the supervision of the share system, which was described as "slavery under a new name." This sudden growth of cash tenancy, however, reflected no credit whatever on the negro race, and indicated industrial retrogression, not advance. Agriculture reached a very low ebb in the Black Belt in the nineties, when, added to the other trials of the employers of labor, a prolonged period of depression afflicted the cotton South.[14] The immediate effect of this depression (cotton fell below five cents) was to impel more farmers to give up farming and to accelerate the townward movement. Renters were naturally substituted for share hands under these circumstances. Many small farmers lost their holdings in this decade, being sold out by merchant creditors. These new owners rented to negroes and looked to the supply end of the business for their profits. It is true that the negro gained a little more personal freedom by the change, but at the same time he sacrificed his best opportunity for economic advancement. His position as a renter was indeed a hard one. He could not afford to purchase efficient stock, improved implements and high-grade fertilizers; he was either not alive to the agricultural changes going on about him, or, knowing of the new methods, he was unable to introduce them.[15] This extension of renting became so marked that resident planters found it almost impossible to secure laborers. In many cases known to the writer, farmers had to draw on the negro population of the towns, hauling them six or seven miles, to and from the fields every day.

At the close of the period of depression it is interesting to have expert testimony as to the effect of this renting. The Commis-

---

[14] *Report of the Industrial Commission,* 1900, X., pp. 445, 458.
[15] *Reports on Georgia Plantation Districts,* Report no. 8, pp. 3, 4.

sioner of Agriculture, testifying before the Industrial Commission, stated:[16]

"We think the tenant system as a whole has a tendency to reduce the
average production per acre of most of our crops, because a great deal
is left to the management of the unintelligent negro farm hand, the
landlord being interested to only the extent of his rent."

To the same effect was the testimony of a Connecticut man, who
had come to Houston County to engage in the peach industry.
In his opinion it was a mistake to suppose the negro to be an
inferior laborer.   He had never had as good workers in New
England.   The real difficulty in the agricultural situation, as he
saw it, lay in the circumstance that

"There is too little of the owner's direct management, because with
the renting and tenancy there is the tendency I spoke of before, of half-
way work, neglect to look after it."

The result of this sort of farming may be gathered from the
statistical tables.[17]   The *per capita* of wealth for both whites and
blacks is low.   In fourteen of the counties of the Belt the value of
farm lands is below ten dollars per acre.[18]   In only two counties
does the average value come within the twenty-five to fifty dollar
class, while in the much smaller Upper Piedmont there are nine
such counties.   In cotton production, the output of the Black
Belt has at each decade been a smaller part of the total for the
state,[19] declining from 82.87 per cent. in 1860 to 57.98 in 1910,
while the per acre product keeps steadily behind that of the
white sections north and south of the Belt.

A great change has been coming over the Black Belt in the last
decade.   The high price of cotton between 1900 and 1910; the
stimulus to better methods resulting from the activity of the
College of Agriculture; the noteworthy improvement in the
roads since the convict lease system was abolished and the prison-
ers began to be used on the public roads; and the bettering of
rural schools have contributed to reawaken the interest of Black

---

[16] *Report of the Industrial Commission*, 1900, X, 379, 907.
[17] See Table, *ante*, p. 70.
[18] See Map, *post*, p. 129.
[19] See Table, *post*, p. 124.

Belt landowners in farming. In some counties the tide of white migration to towns has been checked. The result has been a general improvement in rural conditions. Many facts may be adduced to show the truth of this statement. The value of all farm property in the state increased in the last decade 154.2 per cent. against 32.2 per cent. in 1880–1890, and 20.7 per cent. in 1890–1900.[20] The average value of farm lands and buildings per acre advanced from $6.95 in 1900 to $17.78 in 1910, while the average value of land alone increased 167.4 per cent. Furthermore, while there was a decrease of 21.2 per cent. in the number of acres per farm, the improved acreage increased 15.8 per cent. These figures are for the state as a whole, but all sections participated in the appreciation of values. This revival of agriculture has had a most significant influence on land tenure in the Black Belt. Between 1890 and 1900 renters increased from 26.08 per cent. of the whole body of farmers to 40.54 per cent., while share tenants declined from 38.23 per cent. to 29.36 per cent. During the last decade, however, while cash tenancy barely holds its own, the bulk of the new farms are share tenants' holdings, this class of farmers not declining in numbers as in the preceding decade, but growing from 29.36 to 32.96 per cent. of the whole. The meaning of this change is that supervision on the part of owners is increasing.[21] Planters all over the Belt are alive to this change, and they are unanimous in holding that it means a return to better farming methods. The change is especially noteworthy in the case of negroes. For the first time, comparative data by races at two census periods is available. The table above shows that while renting has increased to some extent among whites, the percentage of negro renters declined during the decade, while there was a slight increase of share tenants. Inquiry on the ground brought out the fact that the resident planters were the first to change the system of tenancy. On plantations operated with a mixed laboring force of wage hands, croppers, and renters, the tendency has been strong to reduce the number of renters, even though it entailed letting the land lie idle. Many planters intend to displace all renters as rapidly as possible. The feeling

---

[20] U. S. Census, 1910, Bulletin : *Agriculture in Georgia*, pp. 4, 5.
[21] *Reports on Georgia Plantation Districts*, Report no. 8, p. 4 ; no. 9, p. 3 ; no. 6, p. 4.

is that lands which are increasing in value at so great a rate cannot longer be allowed to remain in inefficient hands.[22]

In some counties, an interesting compromise is being tried, looking to a combination of the best features of renting and share farming.[23] Possibly the most important objection the average negro has to the share system is that the landlord owns the work animal used by the tenant and refuses to allow indiscriminate use of the animal for riding purposes. Where an animal is available, it is the negro's custom to spend his nights and Sundays riding over the country, attending "revival" meetings, which frequently last months, lodge meetings, and other festivities. This use of work animals cannot be tolerated by the owners, and consequently the cropper feels his social activities curtailed. As a renter, he has possession of a mule to maltreat as he will. The terms of the conventional cropping arrangement are that the landlord shall furnish land, house, mule and its feed, all implements, half the fertilizers, and supply the tenant; the cropper furnishes all the labor, half the fertilizers and receives half the crop after the charges for supplies advanced have been deducted. Under the new arrangement, when the prospective tenant owns his mule and tools, the landlord furnishes the land, house, feed for mule, and all the fertilizers. This compromise is being rapidly adopted. From the standpoint of the landlord, the advantages of the change are that he can use plenty of commercial manures and can make sure that the work animal receives sufficient food to maintain working efficiency. Both are important points. The average renter cannot be induced to use a profitable amount of fertilizers, because he is unconvinced of the wisdom of so doing, while his mule frequently breaks down from sheer starvation. The third and most important advantage to the landlord is that he retains the right of supervision of the cropper's work as under the former arrangement.

From the point of view of the tenant, the most important advantage lies in the securing of an animal for riding purposes; if he has no mule, the planter sells him one on long time payments. Furthermore, the tenant escapes the onerous burden of paying

---

[22] *Ibid,* no. 3, p. 3.
[23] *Ibid,* no. 5, pp. 2, 3 ; no. 6, p. 4.

for fertilizers, while reaping the profit of the owner's investment in that direction.

Absentee merchants and landlords have also moved against the irresponsible renter. A curious situation has come about in some of the most important Black Belt counties. Absentees, seeing that their lands were becoming impoverished under the renting system, have turned over their plantations on long time leases to a class of capitalist-merchants. These merchants have organized the cotton industry on a scale not hitherto practiced in Georgia. One such merchant[24] operates 22,000 acres, half of which he rents from other owners. Except for a scattering handful on the outskirts of the several places, the renters have been dispensed with on this large tract of land, being replaced by croppers and wage hands. The tract is divided into eight or ten plantations, each with a resident manager, who directs all farming operations. In addition to the managers, the merchant employs two "riders," who spend their entire time in the saddle, going over the crops of the tenants and reporting on their condition to the head office in the county town. The merchant operates in this town a large supply business. Reports of the riders are the basis of credit at the store. All tenants are required to buy exclusively from the landlord, and the amount of their credit depends on the condition of their crops. If the crop be neglected, credit is restricted or stopped until the place is put in order.

This is an efficient system from the standpoint of production and soil conservation. It has a tendency, however, to dissuade absentees from dividing and selling their lands, and consequently discourages the growth of small ownership. The counties where this form of organization is practiced are steadily becoming blacker in population. The small farmers from North and Middle Georgia pass over these counties and go on into the Wiregrass further south.

All over the Black Belt, and especially in the lower section, the evils attendant upon absentee landlordism are being greatly lessened by a new method of supervision. A few years ago absentees were unable to give any regular attention to their tenants

[24] *Plantation Schedules, 1911*, no. 40. *Reports on Georgia Plantation Districts*, Report no. 4, p. 4.

because of the distance between town and plantation and the condition of the country roads, but now with the transformation in the condition of the roads, landowners are buying automobiles. Owners with this quick method of transportation run out daily to their farms, spend the day in the work of supervision, and return to their families at night. This development is conspicuous in Southwest Georgia. Many large landowners reside in Albany, Americus, Dawson, Bainbridge and other towns, and their plantations apparently suffer but little from the fact of their non-residence on them. It would be difficult to find anywhere farms more excellently operated.

The agrarian revolution of the post-bellum period has, of course, been more profound and conspicuous in the Black Belt than elsewhere in the State, since it was there that the dominant type of ante-bellum industrial organization had its most complete sway. But the plantation did not by any means totally disappear. Here and there in every county one meets with highly organized large-scale farms, and the movement that appears to be under way from cash renting to share farming seems to indicate an extension of the plantation system, since share tenants are rarely found on any other than efficiently supervised plantations. Such a plantation may be worth describing in detail.[25] The plantation selected as a type of the best class is in one of the oldest of the Black Belt counties, and the soil has been cultivated for many years. The present owners are two young men, both of whom live on the place, giving their entire time to the work of supervision. The total acreage is 3,750, of which 2,500 acres are improved. The two residences of the owners, set in a fine oak grove, are modern structures, with every convenience, such as screens, waterworks, and acetylene lights. Back of the residences are four large barns, in which all the stock used on the plantation are housed and fed, two tool sheds, a blacksmith shop, a commissary, a gas plant, automobile garage, hothouse, dairy building, and several model chicken houses. There are two artesian wells.

Scattered over the plantation at convenient places are the

---

[25] Plantation Schedules, 1911, no. 8.

tenant houses, eighty-six in number.   All are comparatively new
frame structures, costing on the average $300.00.   No log houses
were seen.

The farm equipment includes a large assortment of tools and
machinery, gang plows, disk plows and harrows, McCormick and
Deering reapers and binders, mowing machines, and the like.

The stock and other animals were as follows: 80 mules, 5
horses, 1 ox, 8 milch cows, 150 head of hogs, and about 1500
chickens.

The plantation population includes a white overseer, 15
renters, 90 share tenants, and 3 day laborers, all negroes.   The
renters pay as rental 1,000 pounds of lint cotton for twenty acres,
the laborers are paid $12.00 per month and board, the share
hands get one-half the crop.

As to the general method of farming, the owner's principal
interest is cotton raising, but he produces all the corn and hay
used on the place.   Rotation is practiced as extensively as practicable in view of the fact that each year the major part of the
acreage is devoted to cotton.   All the land is broken in the fall
with two- and four-horse plows, large quantities of fertilizers are
used ($18,000 worth in 1910), and cultivation is frequent.

The products in 1910 were as follows: 1,000 bales of cotton on
1725 acres, 15,000 bushels of corn on 600 acres, 3,900 bushels of
oats on 75 acres, 125 tons of peavines on the same 75 acres.

The owners have no other business and own no land except
this plantation.   Their entire time is given to supervision.
They believe supervision to be indispensable.   "If they should
turn over their plantation to the negroes they would have nothing
in two years."   The nature of the oversight is seen in these facts.
All of the 105 laborers are under the direct control of the owners.   No distinction is made in this regard between renters
and croppers.   The acreage of each crop is regulated, every
tenant goes to work and 'knocks off' at tap of bell, all products
are marketed by the owners.   Nothing is left to the judgment of
the tenant—absolute control is exercised with respect to the use
and application of fertilizers, terracing, clearing and opening of
ditches, repairing of roads and fences, depth and direction of
plowing, time and method of planting, cultivating and harvest-

ing.   The owners felt that this control was best for them, for the land, and for the tenants.   They believed that a supervised cropper would be more likely to have profits for investment in land than an unsupervised renter.

Advances are made to tenants in the form of cash, ten per cent. being charged to all accounts at the end of the year.   Tenants buy their supplies where they please, the commissary being kept for their convenience.   Tenants are allowed the use of animals for riding purposes, but this privilege is by permission in every instance, and is regarded as a return for faithful work.

Every one of the tenants in 1910 paid his account.   Twelve share tenants cleared more than $300 each, after all expenses were paid.   One renter cleared $900 on a two-horse farm.   He had a large family to help him.   All of these profits, the owner said, were squandered.   Even the renter whose profits were so large returned at Christmas to borrow a few dollars for the holidays.   Tenants throw away their money on buggies, fine harness, guns, clothes.   Peddlers have given a great deal of trouble, selling negroes at exorbitant prices cabinet organs, patent medicines, clocks, and other unnecessary articles.

The tenants habitually drink, gamble, and carry weapons. Venereal diseases and consumption were reported as prevalent.

Some of the newer tendencies in the Black Belt are indicated in the following letter, dated February, 1912, and written by an Oglethorpe County planter of long experience.[26]

"Several years ago there were a great many more negro tenants in our county here than whites.   We still have more negroes than whites in Oglethorpe, but the whites are increasing, not many moving away. . . . [The negroes] are better tenants and workers now than a few years ago, and are in sharp competition with the white tenants.   In some sections of our county white colonies have come in and bought from 25 to 50 acres to the farm and are beginning to farm on the intensive system.   Land even without regard to cotton is advancing in price all the time.   There are some counties above us with large and increasing white population, and the overflow is coming down in our county and the counties below.   Madison county adjoining us [on the north] has a large white population, small farms, and I think now holds a better position than Oglethorpe. . . . I have on my home farm

---

[26] *Inquiries I,* 1912, Letter from Oglethorpe County.

five white families and eight negro families. . . . I rented most of my land in 1911 for one-fourth of all crops, cotton, corn, wheat, oats, pease. Every man has his garden, potato and melon patches entirely free. I am adopting the one-fourth system for the purpose of inducing my tenants to diversify and rotate their crops. . . . I also rent every tenant a few acres of bottom land, thoroughly set in Bermuda, so that every tenant will have hay for his stock. I keep myself about seventy-five head of cattle, feed them in the winter on cotton seed meal and hulls, keep them in stalls, save all the manure, and have the tenants near my home use this manure on the land about my house. . . . This land makes a bale of cotton, 450 pounds lint to the acre, and in 1911, the greatest cotton year I have seen in my life, some acres made two bales. . . . Under the late tendency of things our lands that just ten or fifteen years ago were from six to ten dollars per acre are now worth from twenty to seventy-five dollars. . . ."

This letter is an important one. The statements made in it have been repeated by other correspondents, and the writer has personally visited Oglethorpe and other counties on the border of Group II, where these changes are going on. There is a marked tendency towards intensive culture, diversification and rotation, greater attention to tenants, and the result is seen in the increased product per acre and the enhanced value of farm lands. The most interesting point in the letter is the statement in regard to the coming of whites to Oglethorpe. The same thing is true of Greene, Morgan and other counties of the neighborhood. It will be noted that the correspondent drew a comparison between Madison County and Oglethorpe. Madison is one of Group II, treated in the preceding chapter. The movement of small farmers from Group II to the Black Belt is a fact of unusual interest. The high type of farming practiced in the northern counties has sent the price of land up so high that small owners are finding it profitable to sell out, move to the Black Belt and buy there two or three acres for the price received for one. Fifty years ago the fathers of these farmers were moving in the other direction, from the high priced Black Belt cotton lands to the cheap and undesirable Upper Piedmont soil. Three new settlements of whites are now to be found in Oglethorpe County, and in most of the Black Belt counties one meets with recent comers from North Georgia. Many of them become tenants for a few years. The Census of 1910 showed that there were about 4,000 more white tenants in the Belt than in 1900. It is probable that most of these were migrants from North Georgia, since there are virtually no white day laborers from whom the tenant class may be recruited. The 20,000 new negro tenants were former day laborers.

Some difference of opinion was found with reference to the desirability of the white tenant. Complaint was heard that they have difficulty in learning to grow cotton, that they are inclined to be less tractable than negroes, that they make demands for better housing. One planter-merchant naïvely confessed that his principal objection to white tenants was that they did not spend their profits so freely at his store as did the negroes.[27] The majority of planters, however, welcome the white tenant; and their demand for better homes is being met by the erection of a superior type of tenant houses.[28] Planters state that they find the white tenant more intelligent and trustworthy, that they save their profits, become landowners, and thus give stability to Black Belt social conditions. In South Georgia, as well as in Oglethorpe County, the negro tenants are said to be improving as workers as a result of white competition. A Thomas County planter said:[29]

"North Georgia people are having considerable effect on the quality of negro labor. Renters have given better satisfaction this year than ever before, and I attribute it to the fact that whites are coming in and lands are being divided. I told my renters that unless they did better, I would be obliged to sell and they would have nowhere to go. Many planters are dispensing with negroes and putting in white people. Some of the sensible darkies are seeing that they are going to be pushed out."

This emergence of a class of white tenants and small white owners in the Black Belt is fortunate. Thoughtful observers say that the race problem in the Belt is largely the outcome of the negroes' numerical ascendency, and that any movement tending to increase the proportion of whites to blacks can but have a good result.

---

[27] *Reports on Georgia Plantation Districts,* Report no. 3, p. 6.
[28] *Plantation Schedules,* no. 32.
[29] *Plantation Schedules,* no. 17.

Throughout the Black Belt the tenant and laboring class of negroes are improvident. Books of employers indicate that the average tenant makes a profit from his farming. It is the exceptional negro, however, who saves anything. In numerous cases, they squander in a month enough cash to supply them the entire following year, thus heedlessly throwing away the opportunity to escape from exorbitant time prices and from the position of debtors. As a general thing the surplus melts away without any substantial return. Whiskey, gambling, indulgence in sexual pleasures, purchase of useless articles of luxury, and excursions to distant towns, absorb their profits. Tenants usually spend all of the proceeds of the year's work before Christmas and return to the landlord for small sums to tide them over the holiday season. The writer cannot recall an instance of a planter who had not found it necessary to make such advances. He usually has no option in the matter. Contracts are made yearly and expire with the harvest season. "Christmas money" is commonly advanced on the agreement of the tenant to renew his contract for another year. It is said that the landlord who would refuse to make these advances would very likely be unable to secure tenants.

A school and church are to be found on practically every plantation. Great interest is taken by the negroes in the church, as it is the centre of their social life. A lodge or secret society usually meets in the church. The schools are always taught by negroes and are of a uniformly low standard. Attendance is fitful and confined to the late summer and winter months. During the busy season negro children are used in chopping, and later in picking, cotton.

The moral conditions existing among the blacks appear to vary with the proportion they form of the total population. The larger the plantation, the fewer the whites, the greater the distance from civilizing influences, the worse become the conditions. On an immense plantation of sixteen thousand acres, the manager said he had found it impossible to prevent gambling and drinking. Although the plantation was eighteen miles from a town, a plentiful supply of cheap whiskey was provided by pedlars. The manager also expressed a doubt whether there was a man or woman on the plantation untainted by syphilis. The same conditions were reported on the plantation above described in detail. A Crisp County planter "has a terrible amount of trouble with syphilis and consumption among his tenants." Even the best ordered place the writer visited, where the owner and his wife periodically collected the men and women separately and talked to them on the subject, doing everything possible to encourage chastity and fidelity, the planter was obliged to confess failure, and to say "the negroes have no conception of the meaning of sexual purity."[30]

In one county a prominent farmer had served on a grand jury committee to investigate the alleged shipments of whiskey to negroes from points outside the state (Georgia is a prohibition state) and ascertained from the records of the railroad that in one spring five hundred barrels of whiskey had been received, consigned to negroes living in the country districts. It seems that the cars would be shifted to a sidetrack, the doors left open, and negroes would drive in from considerable distances by night and cart the whiskey away. This farmer found eighty quart bottles of whiskey in one of his tenant houses.

Another habit to which the negroes are addicted is that of carrying concealed weapons. Two or three years ago the legislature passed an act requiring that every person before possessing a pistol should secure a license and obtain personal surety that no improper use be made of the weapon. Under cover of this law, a Terrell County planter with a constable went the rounds of his tenant houses and collected twenty-eight pistols, which he holds until the tenants comply with the law.

The presence of many mulatto children in the state is popularly supposed to indicate illicit intercourse between white men and negro women. Special inquiry was made on this point. It was frequently pointed out that mulatto men almost never marry black women, and that the mulatto children are born to mulatto parents. Practically every farmer interviewed during the summer of 1911 was decidedly of the opinion that this relation between white men and negro women had almost entirely ceased. An elderly planter said that the change in sentiment in

---

[30] *Ibid,* nos. 8, 10, 24, 25, 28, 31. 33.

this regard in the past twenty years amounts to a revolution.[31] Once or twice the opinion was expressed in towns that the evil was still prevalent, but as a rule town people agreed with the planters that a great change had taken place.

The physical surroundings of the negro tenant houses are wretched in the extreme. No pride whatever is usually taken in keeping the home neat and clean and the premises attractive. Occasionally one sees a well-kept garden spot, but as a rule weeds hold sway between house and field. Efforts to interest tenants in truck gardens and poultry are in most cases utter failures. Land is always given for gardens and patches, and often the seed is furnished, but no results are obtained. It would be a comparatively easy matter for tenants to raise much of their foodstuffs, if they had the inclination to do so. Their failure to take advantage of this opportunity is not due to lack of time. Negro tenants invariably take Saturdays off. Every Black Belt town is crowded on that day. It is an astonishing fact to relate, but many farmers do a regular business selling to their negro tenants cabbage, potatoes, chickens and the like, when the tenant could easily, without any cost whatever except an occasional hour's work, provide himself with every country product.

---

[31] *Ibid,* no. 39.

CHAPTER VII

THE WIREGRASS COUNTRY AND THE COAST COUN-TIES: ECONOMIC HISTORY AND LAND TENURE MOVEMENTS

A. THE WIREGRASS COUNTRY

The division marked out on the map[1] as the Wiregrass, or Group IV, occupies the southeastern section of Georgia. Not all of the counties lying in what is known as the Wiregrass country are included in this group, a number of the border counties having been placed in the Black Belt, because of the fact that the majority of the population was colored. All of the counties of Group IV have white majorities.

This group of counties is a part of the coastal plain of Georgia, and hence for the most part the elevation above sea level is not great, ranging from one hundred feet to five hundred on the northern border. The surface of the ground is usually level, though occasionally slightly rolling. It presents to the eye an unrelieved expanse of pine forests, carpeted with wiregrass. The soil is a fine sand, often ten to fifteen inches deep, underlaid with yellow clay. Malarious lakes and swamps abound, and, until artesian wells became common, health conditions were bad.[2]

Though the Wiregrass only recently began to attract a large population, some of the counties were laid out at an early period, such as Montgomery, in 1793; Bulloch, in 1796; and Emanuel, in 1812. The soil was thought to be hopelessly sterile. Indeed, the country was known until a few years ago as "the Pine Barrens." The only settlers who came to this region were those attracted by the fine grazing for cattle. The early population consisted of

---

[1] See *post*, p. 127.
[2] *Georgia Historical and Industrial*, p. 162.

typical frontiersmen, from the Carolinas and various parts of
Georgia. After the manner of the frontier, these people lived on
the products of their herds, on game, and cornbread. They were
ignorant and illiterate. The population was very sparse. In 1820
the county of Irwin had only 411 inhabitants,[3] notwithstanding
the fact that it embraced all the land now divided into seven
counties. The total population of the twenty counties of the
group in 1870 was 84,333, of which 70 per cent. was white.[4] At
that census the density of the population was five to the square
mile; in 1880, the density had advanced to seven; and in 1890 to
thirteen per square mile.[5] The sparseness of the population was
due to the fact that the Wiregrass was outside the path of the cotton planter in ante-bellum days, while the bulk of the small farmers were in the region north of the Black Belt. Few negroes
found their way into the Wiregrass until very recent times.
With the improvement in health conditions, due principally to
artesian water, and with the spread of cotton production, made
possible by the liberal use of commercial manures, population has
grown rapidly, and many negroes have migrated to the region.
In 1910 they were 38.4 per cent. of the population.

The Wiregrass is the great yellow pine region of the state. By
1890 the lumber and turpentine industries were attracting capital and people.[6] Farming interests advanced at the same time.
In the decade between 1890 and 1900 about one hundred thousand
new settlers came to the region. Eight new counties have been
laid off in the group since 1900, and many of the towns have had a
rapid growth. In 1910 the population of the group was 460,341,
an increase of 445.8 per cent. since 1870.

Railroads have done much to develop the Wiregrass country.
Up to the time of the Civil War no railroads were to be found in
this large section of Georgia. The first line to pierce the group
was the Savannah, Albany and Gulf, which was completed
through the lower part of the region in 1867; and in 1869 the Macon and Brunswick was finished, running through the heart of

---

[3] Smith, *Story of Georgia*, p. 321. As late as 1866, Mr. Smith rode seventeen
miles on a public road through this county without coming to a house.

[4] See Table *ante*, p. 70.

[5] Harper, R. M., in Savannah *Morning News*, April 16, 1911.

[6] *Ibid.*

the section.   Since the seventies, many main lines and branches have gridironed the Wiregrass country, and there are now some fifteen hundred miles of railway in the group.

The land tenure statistics for the Wiregrass are as follows:

LAND TENURE IN GROUP IV[7]
ALL FARMERS

Year	All farms.	Per cent. of all farms in state	Operated by owners	Cash tenants	Share tenants
1880...................	13,609	9.81	80 66	5.77	13.57
1890........	19,758	11.54	70.32	11.30	15.38
1900...................	32,157	14.33	61.34	17.14	21.52
1910...................	53.138	18.24	45.90	20.92	33.15

WHITE FARMERS

Year	All farms.	Per cent. of all farms in state	Operated by owners	Cash tenants	Share tenants
1900...................	24,835	17.51	69.80	12.90	17.30
1910...................	36,495	21.64	57.00	17.48	25.52

NEGRO FARMERS

Year	All farms.	Per cent. of all farms in state	Operated by owners	Cash tenants	Share tenants
1900...................	7,322	8.85	32.64	31.73	35.63
1910...................	16,643	13.58	21.50	28.58	49.92

It is evident that the agricultural development of the Wiregrass had only begun in 1880, as in that year less than ten per cent. of all the farms in Georgia were in the group.   Lands were being advertised by the railroads[8] at extremely low prices: in Pierce county at 25 cents per acre, in Clinch from 50 cents to $1.00, in Lowndes from $1.00 to $5.00.   By 1880 the use of commercial fertilizers had become general, and the sandy soils began to rise in the estimation of cotton producers.[9]   The soil proved to be quite productive when once the proper methods of cultivation became known.

The growth in number of farms was normal up to 1890, but

---

[7] See Table, *post*, p. 123.

[8] Atlantic & Gulf Railroad, *Guide to Southern Georgia and Florida*, 1877.

[9] U. S. Census, VI, 1880, *Cotton Production*, p. 322: "The Pine Barrens [of Georgia] are being settled by people who see that with the aid of fertilizers the poor sandy lands of the region can be made to produce cotton abundantly.   The result is seen in a product per acre somewhat greater than that of the oak and hickory lands of even the more favored metamorphic region."

after that time very rapid, increasing 62 per cent. in the decade from 1900 to 1910. Nearly a fifth of all farms in the state are now in this group of counties. The new farmers are said to come principally from the mountain counties of North Georgia. Inasmuch as the mountain county farms have declined from 11.43 per cent. of all farms in 1880 to 7.85 per cent. in 1910, the statement would seem to be correct.

The percentage of farms operated by owners has declined steadily. It is not difficult to find the explanation of this fact. Lands in South Georgia were distributed in lots of larger size than elsewhere in the state,[10] often running as high as 490 acres, and the individual holdings have always been larger than in other parts of Georgia. As long as grazing and lumbering were the principal industries, the tendency was for holdings to remain large, or even to increase in size. Many thousands of acres often got into the hands of a single individual or company.[11] But as soon as the earlier industries began to wane and agriculture to increase in importance, the tenant class emerged. Many former lumbermen and turpentine farmers became agriculturists, not selling to their former laborers, but retaining them as tenants. This process is still going on. A Bulloch county farmer reports his "plantation" as containing 14,000 acres, but has only thirty tenants. Inquiry elicited the information that 11,500 acres of this holding were pine forests. Turpentining and sawmilling are going on in one part of the "plantation," farming in the other.[12] The farming interest increases every year, with the gradual clearing of the land, and eventually the entire tract will be devoted to cotton production. This process involves a large increase in the number of tenants, but no dimunition in the number of land owners, the percentage of farms operated by owners, however, becomes progressively smaller with the extension of agriculture. In 1880, tenants were 19.34 per cent. of all farmers, in 1910, 44.10 per cent., but the absolute number of farms operated by owners increased from 10,976 to 24,387.

---

[10] Banks, *op. cit.*, p. 42.

[11] Some of these huge holdings are still intact. In Emanuel County an elderly planter who has lived in the county since the Civil War, owns 30,000 acres. See *Reports on Georgia Plantation Districts*, Report no. 4, p. 7.

[12] *Plantation Schedules*, 1911, no. 11.

Two avenues leading to ownership have been open to the small farmer. In the first place, many lumber and turpentine companies, on the decline of those industries, did not care to engage in farming, and consequently threw their holdings on the market at low prices. The small owner of North Georgia, or the successful tenant, could easily acquire a farm in the Wiregrass country, and thousands took advantage of the opportunity. In the second place, peculiar conditions have attracted a superior type of tenants, who have evolved more quickly into owners than is usually the case. A large part of the area of the group is covered with stumps and small pines left by the sawmill. The main problem of the owner is to get the land cleared for cultivation. The general method is to turn over such lands to white tenants rent free for a term of three or four years, on condition that each year a given amount of clearing be done. The whites who take advantage of this opportunity are North Georgians with sufficient capital to stock a farm, but not enough to purchase land. This type of tenant farmer is not only himself a laborer, but is a manager of labor. On such an undeveloped holding in Emanuel county, the tenant population consisted of fifteen whites and seven negroes. Twelve white renters, some of whom operated as high as eight plows, had between them forty-three sub-tenants and laborers, and owned fifty-two mules. The owner stated that several of these whites had money to buy land, and would do so as soon as their contracts with him had expired.[13]

In the study of Group II, the Upper Piedmont, it was shown that there had been since 1870 a striking development of cotton growing. The same development has occurred in the Wiregrass. The causes have been the same, the increasing importance of the small white farmer, and the use of commercial fertilizers on land formerly thought to be unsuited to cotton culture. In 1870, only 3.87 per cent. of the total product of the state was produced in this section; in 1910, 18.67 per cent. The acreage increased from 5.06 per cent. of the whole in 1880 to 16.79 per cent. in 1910. The per acre product in 1910 was .454 bales, far ahead of the other two large groups.[14]

[13] *Ibid*, no. 12.
[14] See *post*, p. 124.

The preponderance of white farmers seems to have the same fortunate effects on the tenant class that were noted in the case of the Upper Piedmont. Almost every planter visited by the writer in the summer of 1911 reported that his tenants were saving money.[15] An Emanuel county planter stated that all of his tenants were prosperous. There were twenty-two tenants on the place, including six negroes. Five of the six, all share tenants, cleared an average of $250 in 1910. A Bulloch county farmer, employing thirty tenants, all but six of whom were white, reported that all had done well in 1910, except three of the negroes. Practically all saved their profits and were supplying themselves in 1911, without going into debt. A Laurens county farmer with eighteen colored and four white tenants, stated that all of the whites were saving, but only one of the negroes.[16]

A decided preference for the white tenant was often expressed. A noteworthy instance was that of the Laurens county planter who owned five farms, some of which were at a distance from his residence. Formerly all the farms were worked by negro tenants, but they have recently been displaced by whites. The reason given was that the owner found that, on farms so inaccessible as to prevent constant oversight, whites could be trusted to work steadily, whereas negroes could not be so trusted. He stated that the whites were a much better element, saving their money and becoming landowners. From a commercial point of view, the whites were not so profitable (the owner was also a merchant), because they did not spend so freely as did his former black tenants.[17]

Little complaint was heard among Wiregrass farmers of disorder, drunkenness, immorality, or venereal disease among the tenants, white or black.[18] The freedom from these troubles was attributed to the presence of many whites. Only where large numbers of negroes are collected on the plantation, without the presence of whites, was trouble reported. The only planters[19] met with who had had experiences similar to those of Black Belt

---

[15] *Reports on Georgia Plantation Districts,* Report no. 4, p. 6.
[16] *Plantation Schedules,* 1911, nos. 11, 12, 13.
[17] *Ibid,* no. 14.
[18] *Ibid,* nos. 11, 12, 14, 30.
[19] *Ibid,* nos. 13, 23.

planters were a Laurens county farmer who had twenty-five negro laborers and no whites, and a Worth county farmer, all of whose nineteen laborers were negroes. The latter stated that gambling and drinking were prevalent, that it was hard to get his men to work on Saturday or Monday, that venereal diseases were common, and that though all of the tenants cleared money on their farming, none saved anything.

The conviction is strong in the Wiregrass that the negro is a better citizen when he lives in a largely white community. That this is the case seems probable from the fact that 21.50 per cent. of the negro farmers operate their own farms, against 9.13 per cent. in the Black Belt, and that the per capita wealth of the negroes is $31.27, as compared with $23.75 in the other section.

B. THE COAST COUNTIES

The coast region of six counties covers an area of about two thousand square miles.[20] It includes "savannas," live oak lands, coast tide swamp lands, and islands.

The savannas occupy most of the area of the six counties. They are a belt of meadow-like land from ten to fifteen miles in width, less than fifteen feet above tide-water. The western limit of this belt is the wiregrass bluff, ranging from twenty-five to fifty feet above sea level. The savannas are covered with a sparse growth of long-leaf pine and a thick undergrowth of saw-palmetto.

The live-oak lands spread along the coast and the islands. The soil is yellow and mulatto sand. Immense live-oaks, festooned with streamers of gray moss, are the most noteworthy characteristic of the coast region. Some of the live-oak lands are rich, having a blue clay subsoil well adapted to sea-island cotton.

Several of the large rivers of the state, the Savannah, the Ogeechee, the Altamaha, and the St. Mary's, find their way to the ocean through the coast counties. Along the banks of these rivers, ranging from ten to twenty miles, lie the coast tide swamp lands. These swamp lands formerly produced large quantities of rice.

---

[20] *Georgia Historical and Industrial,* pp. 165–166.

The sea-islands, about five hundred and sixty square miles in total area, form a network along the coast. They are some fifteen feet above sea-level, have a sandy soil, suitable for sea-island cotton and diversified crops, though very little farming is done on them.

Beginning with the settlement of Savannah in 1733, the coast was occupied during the middle of the eighteenth century by successive colonies of English, Scotch, German, and Swiss immigrants. One important colony of New Englanders settled in what is now Liberty county. These immigrants were scattered about in numerous villages, many of which have wholly disappeared.[21] During the first twenty years of the colony an effort was made to establish something resembling the New England economy of small farms grouped about villages. Slavery was prohibited, and the area of land each settler might have was strictly limited, with the view of preventing the growth of large estates. From the first, however, the colonists were dissatisfied with the rules of the trustees of the colony.[22] They claimed that the heat and the swampy, malarious nature of the country made sustained physical exertion on the part of white men impossible, and that they were unable to compete in the markets of the world with South Carolina, where slavery was allowed. Petition after petition was sent to the trustees, praying that the restriction as to slavery be removed. It was further asserted that fifty acres of land was too small a tract for practical purposes, especially in view of the fact that part of the holding might be swampy and unavailable for agricultural purposes.

After resisting the pressure for twenty years, the trustees finally yielded, and slavery was introduced in 1751. The coast immediately began to develop. The tide of population which had started away from the colony was checked, and many new settlers came. With one exception, the seaboard counties had black majorities by 1790. At the close of the ante-bellum period, the coast was the region of largest slaveholdings in the state. The average was twenty per owner (for the state, the average was

---

[21] Jones, C. C., *Dead Towns of Georgia, passim.*
[22] Stevens, W. B., *History of Georgia* (New York 1847), I., chaps. VIII and IX.

eleven), and more than one-fourth of all the owners of one hundred or more slaves were in these six counties.[23]

With the introduction of slavery, social differentiation took place. The poorer element was obliged to leave the richer regions along the river banks. Many drifted into the pine barrens of the coast and into the nearest tier of Wiregrass counties. The upper class developed into the planter type. The social prestige and political power of the coast planter were marked. The poorer folk were wholly illiterate and sustained themselves with difficulty on the infertile soil of the pine barren lands.[24]

Rice growing was the principal interest of the sea-coast planter. Many of these plantations were very large and extremely productive. Travellers have left descriptions of several of them.[25] The rice planter as a rule lived on his plantation only in winter. As soon as the warm weather approached, he retreated to a more salubrious climate, leaving the plantation in the hands of an overseer.[26] Absenteeism, the absolute power of the overseer, his low moral standards, and the crowding together of many negroes, brought about more unfortunate conditions on the coast than were to be found elsewhere in the state. The coast negroes were said to have been less intelligent and capable than those of the up-country.

Civil war and emancipation brought ruin to the coast rice planter. The creation of a rice plantation was an arduous and expensive undertaking. The swamp lands had to be reclaimed and then kept up by constant attention to dikes and canals. Reliable labor was absolutely indispensable. The losses of the up-country planter due to the disorganization of labor were temporary, but the coast planter was obliged to look on in helplessness while his valuable property went to ruin for lack of regular work. Negroes refused to do banking and ditching. Some of the planters attempted to import white labor, but lack of capital

---

[23] U. S. Census, 1860, *Agriculture*, pp. 226–227.

[24] Smith, *Story of Georgia*, pp. 147–148, 149–151.

[25] Olmsted, F. L., *A Journey in the Seaboard Slave States* (New York, 1856), pp. 409–442. Lyell, Sir Charles, *A Second Visit to the United States of North America* (New York, 1849), I, chap. XIX.

[26] Mallard, R. Q., *Plantation Days Before Emancipation* (Richmond, 1892), p. 14.

to repair the ravages of war and the effects of neglect made it impossible to revive the rice industry on a large scale.[27]

One of the finest rice plantations was that of Mr. Hamilton Couper, on the Altamaha river. This plantation was described in detail by Lyell.[28] A son of Mr. Couper in a personal letter to the writer gives an account of his attempt to revive the plantation.[29] He began in 1866, planting on shares with forty or fifty negroes. The experiment was satisfactory, but he gave up the sharing feature, because there was a feeling among the coast planters against making a partner of the negroes, and because the negroes themselves desired to avoid steady work.

"They bought land at a very small price in the adjoining pine woods, and drifted into settlements there. After that they worked for wages either on the rice plantations or wherever wages were to be had: and their labor became unreliable. Yet even under these circumstances the rice planting could have been carried on profitably, had it not been for the hurricanes, which at intervals of some years came at the period of the rice harvest and swept away entire crops. At this date there is only one considerable rice planter left on the Altamaha river . . . In Glynn county the negro has been a failure as a renter, but on wages he has not been a bad laborer on the plantations . . ."

Under such circumstances agriculture retrograded and the seaboard has for many years been in a stationary condition. "Agriculture in Glynn County at present amounts almost to nothing. If ever revived, there must be better drainage and other sanitary precautions, and perhaps new immigration."[30]

The negroes took almost complete possession of the coast in 1865, constituting 73 per cent. of the total population in 1870. In recent years, however, the white element has been rapidly increasing. One of the counties, Bryan, has a white majority, and for the six counties, the percentage of blacks has fallen to 58.6.

The large plantations have disappeared and with them systematized industry. The land has been divided into minute negro-owned farms, and the section has become insignificant in the agriculture of the state.

---

[27] Leigh, *op. cit.*, pp. 263–264.
[28] Lyell, *Second Visit*, I, chap. XIX.
[29] *Inquiries* I, Letter from Glynn County.
[30] *Ibid.*

The stationary condition of farming in the group is indicated in the following table of land tenure.

Land Tenure in the Seacoast Counties[31]

ALL FARMERS

Year	Total farms	Per cent. of all farms in state	Operated by owners	Cash tenants	Share tenants.
1880	4,090	2.95	59.52	30.41	10.07
1890	4,078	2.38	66.46	30.04	3.50
1900	4,532	2.01	76.38	16.22	7.40
1910	4,152	1.42	82.56	10.50	6.94

WHITE FARMERS

1900	1,698	1.20	79.34	10.60	10.06
1910	1,554	.90	77.22	14.99	7.79

NEGRO FARMERS

1900	2,834	3.42	74.60	19.57	5.83
1910	2,608	2.13	82.86	9.85	7.29

There has been practically no increase in the number of farms in thirty years. The breakup of plantations was sudden and complete in the sixties, and since then there has been little change. The thoroughgoing character of the disintegration of plantations is shown in a comparison of the number of farms in the several size groups at the Census periods, 1860 and 1870.

TABLE SHOWING THE DISINTEGRATION OF PLANTATIONS IN THREE TYPICAL SEACOAST COUNTIES

	3–10 acres, 1860–1870		10–20 acres, 1860–1870		20–50 acres, 1860–1870		50–100 acres, 1860–1870		100–200 acres, 1860–1870		500–1,000 acres, 1860–1870		1,000– acres, 1860–1870	
Chatham	24	303	41	207	43	86	28	31	59	44	17	8	3	0
Camden	3	189	5	136	22	53	11	12	36	14	10	4	4	1
Liberty	18	616	35	749	112	366	60	187	104	159	18	2	5	3

Of the fifty-seven plantations of five hundred or more acres, all except eighteen disappeared in the decade. It seems reason-

---

[31] See *post*, p. 123.

ably clear that on the seaboard the disintegration of plantations differed from that of the other sections of the state, in that here it was a real, not a nominal division.   In studying the other groups of counties, the position was taken that the prevalence of the tenant system, especially of the share system, meant that the plantation, in many cases, remained essentially a unit, though the method of collecting data for the census made the tenant's farm appear as a separate holding.   On the seacoast, however, it is to be noted that the tenant system is a negligible factor, and has been of progressively less importance at each census period. Ownership has advanced with great rapidity, each decade witnessing a considerable transference of tenants and laborers to the status of owners.   There is a sharp contrast, therefore, between this and the other groups of counties.   Here at each census period owners have been a larger percentage of all farmers, while elsewhere the percentage of owners has steadily declined.

The average size of the owner-operated farms in 1903 was as follows:[32]

	Whites	Negroes
Bryan	364.1	53.
Camden	47.9	14.9
Chatham	277.3	12.5
Glynn	253.9	27.5
Liberty	356.9	42.9
McIntosh	235.1	20.0

The minute size of the negro farms and the unusual poorness and cheapness of the soil indicate the ease with which negroes have climbed into the class of owners.   A few months' work for wages would suffice to obtain the price of such a patch as the census dignifies with the name of "farm."   The prevalence of ownership in these counties, 82.56 per cent. of all farms being operated by owners, has not served to better agricultural conditions.   The percentage of the land area in farms is lower than in any other section of the state, less than eleven per cent. in

[32] Banks, *op. cit.*, pp. 119–121.

McIntosh County, and in only two counties does the percentage run as high as the forty to sixty class. The per acre value of farm land is as low as in the mountain counties; in only one county (and that Chatham, containing the city of Savannah) is the average within the ten to twenty-five dollar class.[33] Less cotton was produced in 1910 than in 1870, none being reported at the last census for four of the six counties.

The table of *per capita* wealth[34] for this group is of little value as an index of the condition of the agricultural classes, because nearly eighty per cent. of the total property values is in Chatham, and is personal and real property in Savannah. Though negroes constitute 58.6 per cent. of the population of the six counties, and though 82.86 per cent. of their farms are operated by owners, they possess less than 5 per cent. of the property of the group.

---

[33] See Map, *post*, p. 129.
[34] See Table, *ante*, p. 70.

BIBLIOGRAPHY

A. Unpublished Sources.

The latter half of the present work is devoted largely to an account of present-day conditions among the agricultural classes of Georgia. Practically all of the material is unpublished and hitherto unused for historical purposes. The following is a list of the material.

1. Data collected by the writer during the summer of 1911, while acting as Expert Special Agent for the Agricultural Division of the 'Bureau of the Census, in a study of plantation conditions. All the important farming counties of Georgia were visited and systematically studied. Inquiries were made as to the prevalence of the plantation type of organization, the growth and status of small ownership, the several classes of tenancy, and the financial, social and moral conditions of the tenants. Daily reports were sent to the Director of the Census, taking the form of detailed descriptions of individual plantations. Information was obtained from planters, merchants, tenants, and laborers. Duplicates of these reports were retained. These duplicates are in rough form, as they were often obtained under unfavorable conditions. Much of the material is in the shape of shorthand notes, but typewritten transcriptions have been appended wherever quotation has been made. This data, about six hundred pages in all, has been bound and deposited in the library of the University of Georgia, under the title *"Georgia Plantation Schedules, 1911."*

During this investigation, the state was divided into districts of contiguous counties, grouped about convenient centres. On the completion of a district, a report on the district as a unit was made, following an outline prepared by the office of the Chief of Division of Agriculture. Copies of these reports were retained, and have been deposited in the library of the University of Georgia under the title *"Reports on Georgia Plantation Districts, 1911."*

Permission to use this material has been obtained from the Director of the Census.

2. In the winter of 1912 a circular letter was addressed to a number of Georgia planters who had been engaged in agriculture in 1865. The inquiry was not wholly successful, because it was difficult to obtain the names of men whose experience dated back so far; and many of the letters were returned with the note that the addressee was dead. Only twenty-one useful replies were received. Some of the letters, however, went into the matter in considerable detail, giving many useful and interesting facts. These replies have been bound and placed in the library of the University of Georgia, under the title *"Inquiries I, 1912, with reference to farming in Georgia immediately after the Civil War."*

3. For the study of tenancy there are available the results of an investigation conducted in 1902 by the U. S. Department of Agriculture. The value of this inquiry for the present study lies in the occasional supplemental comments by correspondents on the labor situation, and in the answers to questions bearing on the form of tenancy practiced in the several sections of the state. The correspondents were leading farmers. From Georgia 141 replies were received, representing 82 counties. This material was turned over to Dr. Henry C. Taylor, Professor of Agricultural Economics in The University of Wisconsin, and is still in his possession. These letters are designated in the footnotes as *"Inquiries II, 1902."*

4. Supplementary to this inquiry into the tenant system, Professor Taylor undertook, in 1906, to obtain additional information by letter. Only 22 replies came in from Georgia, but they are of value, because of the interest correspondents took in explaining the economic results of the tenant systems. This material may be seen in Professor Taylor's office. The designation here used is *"Inquiries III, 1906."*

B. Published Material.

1. Congressional documents and other publications of the United States government have been the main published source used. The Census publications have been relied on for the

statistical side of the work. Land tenure statistics are now available for four census periods, but it is only since the twelfth Census that data was published separately for white and colored farmers. As has been pointed out in the body of the monograph, the Census method of classification is faulty in that it takes no account of the plantation as such.

U. S. Census, 1880, *Cotton Production in the United States*, VI, contains a valuable account of the status of cotton culture in every county in the State, as well as a description of the soil.

Senate and House *Executive Documents* and *Reports of Committees* have been used for information touching Freedmen's Bureau operations; reports of official emissaries to the South; Ku Klux investigations, and the like.

U. S. Department of Agriculture, *Reports*, 1865 to 1900, and the *Report of the Industrial Commission*, 1900, X, are full of facts bearing on the history of agriculture.

2. Publications of the State of Georgia.

    a. Georgia Legislature, *Acts*, 1865–1910.

    b. Codes of Georgia Laws, 1867, 1873, 1882, 1895, 1911.

    c. Comptroller General of Georgia, *Reports*, 1865–1910. This official is charged with the duty of collecting annual statistics as to property values, improved and wild lands, etc., in every county. Since 1874 this data is available by races.

    d. Supreme Court *Reports*, 1865–1910.

    e. Georgia Department of Agriculture, *Georgia Historical and Industrial*. Atlanta, 1901. A reliable description of the physiography and soils of Georgia, compiled by experts. Contains maps of the soil, temperature, mineral wealth, and geology of the State.

3. Andrews, Sidney. *The South Since the War*. Boston: 1866. Reprint of letters to the Boston *Advertiser* and The Chicago *Tribune*, from a special correspondent who spent fourteen weeks in the South in 1865.

3a. Appleton's *Annual Cyclopedia*, 1865–1872.

4. Banks, E. M. *Economics of Land Tenure in Georgia*. New York: Columbia University Press, 1905. An

analysis from an economist's standpoint of the various forms of land tenure in Georgia. The general thesis is that a return to something like the old plantation system is the solution of the present labor troubles. His view that the Census of 1910 would probably show a decline in share farming was not realized.

5. Brooks, R. P. *Race Relations in the Eastern Piedmont Region of Georgia.* New York: *Political Science Quarterly,* June, 1911.

6. Bruce, P. A. *The Plantation Negro as a Freeman.* New York: G. P. Putnam's Sons, 1889.

7. Campbell, Sir George. *White and Black: the Outcome of a Visit to the United States.* New York: 1879.

8. Carver, T. N. *Principles of Rural Economics.* Boston: Ginn & Co., 1911.

9. DeBow's *Review,* 1865–1870.

10. DuBois, W. E. B. *Negro Landholder of Georgia.* Washington: Department of Labor, Bulletin No. 35, 1901. Contains a series of maps showing the growth and distribution of black population by counties, 1790 to 1890, and tables showing growth of negro property in every county since 1875.

11. Fleming, W. L. *Documentary History of Reconstruction.* Cleveland: The Arthur H. Clark Co., 1907.

12. Georgia Historical Society *Collections,* I, II, Savannah, 1840, 1842. Reprints of many important pamphlets bearing on the early history of the coast counties.

13. Grady, Henry W. *Cotton and Its Kingdom.* New York: Harper's Magazine, October, 1881. Mr. Grady was editor of The Atlanta *Constitution* and had a wide acquaintance with economic conditions in the state. He describes the breakup of the plantations and the rise of the credit system, and its effects on the farmer.

14. Hammond, M. B. *The Cotton Industry.* New York: American Economic Association Publications, New Series, No. 1, 1897. Treats the industrial revolution in the South, the system of agricultural credit, and the prevalent condition of cotton culture. He fails to grasp

the fundamental difference between share farming and renting (See p. 190, footnote). He thought the two systems were alike in their effects on land and production. The authors whom he criticises (Van der Graff and Dillingham) understood the difference between the systems.

15. Hoffman, F. L. *Race Traits and Tendencies of the American Negro.* New York: American Economic Association Publications, XI, 1896. The author expresses strong opinions as to the incapacity of the negro for independent farming.

16. Jones, C. C. *The Dead Towns of Georgia.* Savannah: Morning News Printing Co., 1878. Origin and decline of many of the early settlements in Georgia, especially in the Savannah district.

17. —— *History of Georgia.* Boston: Houghton, Mifflin & Co., 1883. Covers the history of the state through the Revolutionary War.

18. King, Edward. *The Great South.* Hartford: American Publishing Co., 1875.

19. Latham, Henry. *Black and White.* London: 1867. Views of a competent English observer on the social and economic conditions in the South immediately after the War.

20. Leigh, Frances Butler. *Ten Years on a Georgia Plantation Since the War.* London: Richard Bentley & Son, 1883. Mrs. Leigh was the daughter of Frances Anne Kemble, who married a member of the Butler family and went to live on a rice plantation on the Georgia coast. Her *Journal of a Residence on a Georgia Plantation* is a very gruesome picture of slavery. The views of her daughter, Mrs. Leigh, afford an interesting contrast. Mrs. Leigh's work is the most valuable account extant of labor conditions on the coast after the Civil War. Many letters are reproduced. The appendix contains a sketch of the method of rice cultivation.

[511]

21. Nordhoff, Charles. *The Cotton States in the Spring and Summer of 1875.* New York: Appleton & Co., 1876. Valuable comments on economic and social conditions in the South.

22. Peirce, P. S. *The Freedmen's Bureau.* Iowa City: Bulletin of the University of Iowa, March, 1904.

23. Phillips, U. B. *Plantation and Frontier Documents, I and II,* in *Documentary History of American Industrial Society.* Cleveland: The Arthur H. Clark Co., 1909.

24. —— *Georgia and State Rights.* Washington: Government Printing Office, 1902. Political history of Georgia from the Revolution to the Civil War.

25. —— *Origin and Growth of Southern Black Belts.* Washington: American Historical Review, July, 1906. A study of the westward trend of the small farmer, followed by the cotton planter; increase in size of land- and slave-holdings; illustrated by typical case of Crawford County, Georgia.

26. —— *A History of Transportation in the Eastern Cotton Belt to 1860.* New York: Columbia University Press, 1908. Sketches the history of the principal Georgia railways.

27. *South in the Building of the Nation.* Richmond: Southern Historical Society *Publications,* 1909. In volume VI are a number of papers of a general character on the post-bellum economic history of the South.

28. Smith, G. G. *Story of Georgia and the Georgia People.* Atlanta: Franklin Printing and Publishing Co., 1900. Contains reliable and important sketches of the social and economic history of many counties of Georgia.

28a. *Southern Cultivator,* Athens, Ga., 1865–1872.

29. *Southern Recorder,* 1865 to 1872. Milledgeville, Ga. An important Black Belt weekly, published at the former capital of Georgia.

30. Stevens, W. B. *History of Georgia.* New York: Appleton & Co., 1847. 2v.

31. Taylor, H. C. *An Introduction to the Study of Agricultural Economics.* New York: Macmillan Co., 1911.

32. Trowbridge, J. T. *The South.* Hartford: L. Stebbins, 1866. A keen analysis of the southern situation as to agriculture, railways, business, and finance. Judicial throughout.

33. Woolley, E. C. *The Reconstruction of Georgia.* New York: Columbia University Press, 1901. Treats the political side of Reconstruction.

34. Young, Edward, Chief of Bureau of Statistics, Treasury Department. *Special Report on Immigration.* Washington: 1872.

LAND TENURE STATISTICS OF GEORGIA
ALL FARMS

	1880	1890	1900	1910
Total farms	138,626	171,071	224,691	291,211
Operated by owners......	76,451 (55.1)	79,477 (46.4)	81,603 (40.1)	100,231 (34.6)
Cash tenants,.............	18,557 (13.4)	29,413 (17.2)	58,750 (26.2)	82,387 (28.2)
Share tenants............	43,618 (31.5)	62,181 (36.4)	75,810 (33.7)	108,593 (37.2)

WHITE FARMS

	1900	1910
Total farms...	141,865	168,668
Operated by owners..	78,548 (55.4)	84,426 (50.0)
Cash tenants..	24,022 (16.9)	31,908 (18.9)
Share tenants...	39,295 (27.7)	52,334 (31.1)

NEGRO FARMS

	1900	1910
Total farms...	82,826	122,553
Operated by owners..	11,583 (14.0)	15,815 (13.0)
Cash tenants...........	34,728 (42.0)	50,479 (41.1)
Share tenants...	36,515 (44.0)	56,259 (45.9)

LAND TENURE IN GEORGIA¹
ALL FARMS

Year	Group I Total farms	Per cent. of all farms in state	Operated by owners	Tenants Cash	Tenants Share	Group II Total farms	Per cent. of all farms in state	Operated by owners	Tenants Cash	Tenants Share	Group III Total farms	Per cent. of all farms in state	Operated by owners	Tenants Cash	Tenants Share	Group IV Total farms	Per cent. of all farms in state	Operated by owners	Tenants Cash	Tenants Share	Group V Total farms	Per cent. of all farms in state	Operated by owners	Tenants Cash	Tenants Share
1890	15,862	11.43	66.74	2.17	31.09	38,292	27.65	57.70	5.63	36.67	66,778	48.18	45.48	21.00	33.52	13,609	9.81	30.63	5.77	13.57	4,090	2.95	59.52	30.41	10.07
1880	17,652	10.22	61.78	1.91	36.31	44,073	25.76	47.31	7.54	45.14	85,530	50.00	36.00	25.89	38.23	19,254	11.54	73.32	11.30	15.38	4,078	2.38	66.46	30.04	3.50
1900	21,915	9.76	56.60	3.13	40.27	57,841	25.74	47.95	13.73	48.32	108,246	48.16	30.10	40.54	29.36	32,17?	14.33	61.34	17.14	21.52	4,532	2.01	76.38	16.22	7.40
1910	22,869	7.85	54.08	4.39	41.53	73,540	25.24	34.11	17.15	48.74	137,512	47.22	25.48	41.56	32.96	53,138	18.24	45.90	20.92	33.15	4,152	1.42	82.56	10.50	6.94

WHITE FARMS

Year	Group I Total farms	Per cent. of all farms in state	Operated by owners	Tenants Cash	Tenants Share	Group II Total farms	Per cent. of all farms in state	Operated by owners	Tenants Cash	Tenants Share	Group III Total farms	Per cent. of all farms in state	Operated by owners	Tenants Cash	Tenants Share	Group IV Total farms	Per cent. of all farms in state	Operated by owners	Tenants Cash	Tenants Share	Group V Total farms	Per cent. of all farms in state	Operated by owners	Tenants Cash	Tenants Share
1900	20,802	14.60	58.33	3.02	38.65	45,060	31.79	45.70	12.13	42.17	49,470	34.90	54.80	29.40	15.80	24,835	17.51	69.80	12.90	17.30	1,698	1.20	79.34	10.60	10.06
1910	21,631	12.83	55.40	4.30	40.30	55,245	32.76	41.67	14.49	43.84	53,743	31.87	51.00	30.44	18.56	36,495	21.64	57.00	17.48	25.52	1,554	.90	77.22	14.99	7.79

NEGRO FARMS

Year	Group I Total farms	Per cent. of all farms in state	Operated by owners	Tenants Cash	Tenants Share	Group II Total farms	Per cent. of all farms in state	Operated by owners	Tenants Cash	Tenants Share	Group III Total farms	Per cent. of all farms in state	Operated by owners	Tenants Cash	Tenants Share	Group IV Total farms	Per cent. of all farms in state	Operated by owners	Tenants Cash	Tenants Share	Group V Total farms	Per cent. of all farms in state	Operated by owners	Tenants Cash	Tenants Share
1900	1,113	1.24	24.80	5.20	70.00	12,781	15.43	10.73	19.36	69.91	58,776	70.96	9.20	49.90	40.90	7,322	8.85	32.64	31.73	35.63	2,834	3.49	74.60	19.57	5.83
1910	1,238	1.01	30.77	5.81	63.42	18,295	14.93	11.22	25.18	63.60	83,769	68.35	9.13	48.69	42.18	16,643	13.58	31.59	28.58	49.92	2,608	2.13	82.86	9.85	7.29

¹ This table was compiled from preliminary tables in which the statistics for the counties in each group, for each of the four census periods, were brought together. Additions were made on an adding machine and percentages worked out with a slide rule, all the work being verified by the author personally. The forty preliminary tables were then put together in the above tabulation, and it is thought unnecessary to publish them here.

ACREAGE AND PRODUCTION OF COTTON IN GEORGIA.[1]

Year	Group I					Group II					Group III					Group IV					Group V				
	Acreage	Per cent. of total state acreage	Bales	Per cent. state product	Product per acre	Acreage	Per cent. of total state acreage	Bales	Per cent. state product	Product per acre	Acreage	Per cent. of total state acreage	Bales	Per cent. state product	Product per acre	Acreage	Per cent. of total state acreage	Bales	Per cent. state product	Product per acre	Acreage	Per cent. of total state acreage	Bales	Per cent. state product	Product per acre
1860	......	......	4,675	.69	......	......	......	88,670	12.67	......	......	......	581,260	82.87	......	......	......	21,415	3.07	......	......	......	4910	.7	......
1870	......	......	36,421	7.60	......	......	......	52,927	11.27	......	......	......	361,568	76.48	......	......	......	18,344	3.87	......	......	......	3280	.7	......
1880	44,612	1.73	16,246	2.00	.333	523,741	20.01	204,744	25.22	.308	1,912,630	73.06	547,922	67.34	.286	132,415	5.06	42,300	5.29	.319	3740	.14	1230	.15	.329
1890	78,304	2.34	25,328	2.10	.323	716,321	21.42	258,712	21.70	.361	2,304,694	68.89	823,085	69.10	.357	210,942	7.21	83,387	7.00	.346	4843	.14	1334	.10	.275
1900	64,422	1.93	26,762	2.17	.415	786,186	23.52	318,839	25.90	.405	2,253,502	67.4	790,838	64.22	.351	238,077	7.12	94,922	7.71	.398	886	.03	355		.400
1910	94,786	1.94	37,549	1.88	.326	1,039,768	21.28	423,497	21.25	.407	2,921,004	59.82	1,154,964	57.98	.395	819,656	16.79	372,023	18.67	.454	8090	.17	4376	.22	.540

[1] Compiled from tables in U. S. Census Reports, 1860 to 1910.

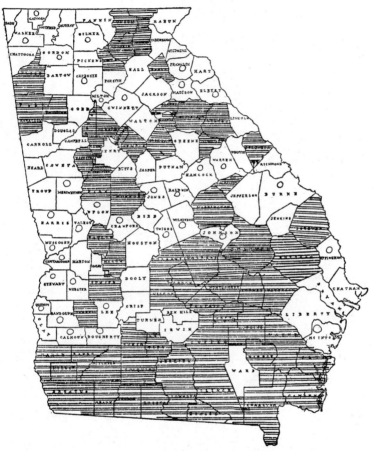

MIGRATION OF WHITES, 1860–1870.

In shaded counties the rate of increase was greater than the rate for the
state, 8.01 per cent. Counties marked O suffered an absolute loss of whites.
See *ante*, p. 15.

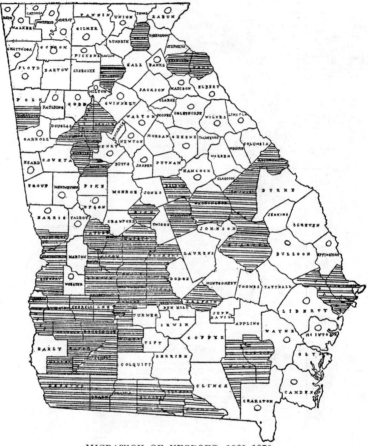

MIGRATION OF NEGROES, 1860–1870.

In shaded counties negroes increased more than average for state. Counties marked O suffered an absolute loss of negro population. Rate of increase for state 17.06 per cent. See *Ante*, pp. 15, 16

THE FIVE SECTIONS OF GEORGIA, WITH PERCENTAGE WHITES
FORMED OF TOTAL POPULATION IN 1910.

See *ante*, pp. 69.

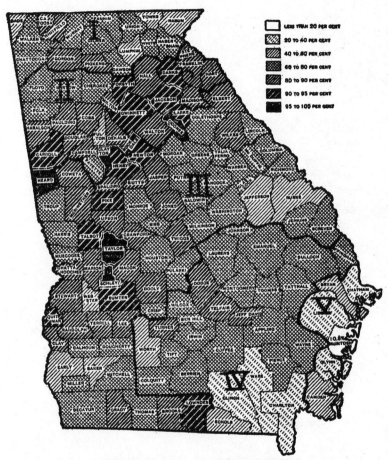

PERCENTAGE OF LAND AREA IN FARMS.

Percentage for the state, 71.7. The percentage of land area in farms, when less than 20, is inserted under the county name.

Reproduction from U. S. Census, 1910. Abstract with Supplement for Georgia, p. 640. The five sections of Georgia (see *ante*, p. 69) have been delimited.

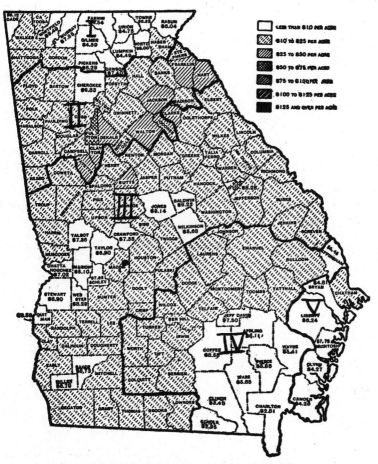

AVERAGE VALUE OF FARM LAND PER ACRE.

Average for the state, $13.74. When the value is less than $10 per acre, it is inserted under the county name.
Reproduced from U. S. Census 1910. Abstract with Supplement for Georgia, p. 640.